# When Supertraders Meet Kryptonite

*Art Collins*

**Traders Press, Inc.®**
**PO Box 6206**
**Greenville, SC 29606**

*Serving Traders since 1975*

**Published by Traders Press, Inc.®**



**ISBN: 0-934380-76-7**



*Teresa Darty Alligood*
*Editor and Graphic Designer*
*Traders Press, Inc.®*

*Cover Designed by Larry Zajac*

**Traders Press, Inc.®**
**PO Box 6206**
**Greenville, SC 29606**

*Serving Traders since 1975*

*To Pat, who personifies the supportive mate lauded within these pages.*

~

*To my daughter Maggi, the light of my life.*

~

*I love you both.*

# Table of Contents

Contents continued...

Contents continued...

Contents continued...

# *Foreword*

## *Ruth Barrons Roosevelt*

All traders experience loss, extended drawdowns, and disastrous days. The only way not to know loss is not to trade. And then you have no gains. It really is a case of nothing ventured, nothing gained.

When Art Collins called me for my story, my first reaction was, "Why are you calling me to hear about loss?"

And yet I had to admit, varying degrees of calamity are part of the extended trading experience. The issues are the following: How do you handle it at the time? How do you manage the memory of it? Do you learn from the experience, or do you repeat it? Do you strengthen yourself through the experience?

By reading this book, by listening to other traders, you can learn that you are not alone. More importantly, you can learn vicariously so that when faced with a similar experience you can act appropriately.

Sometimes when disaster strikes, it has nothing to do with a trader's actions or attitudes. Other times the trader contributes or causes the problem. Over trading in terms of size or frequency, losing focus, wanting to be right, getting caught up in ego, believing a scenario rather than the evidence, fighting the market, and freezing in fear are but a few of the ways a trader can create a mess.

Still, losses occur even when you're trading in a well prepared, disciplined style. I've written it over and over again, so let me say it one more time. Taking a loss does not make you a loser. Taking a bunch of losses does not make you a loser. Refusing to take a loss or doing what doesn't work and doing it over and over again—that makes you a loser.

Read this book, and let the mistakes of others protect you from your own blunders.

**Ruth**

# *Publishers Comments*

In the trading game, learning from the mistakes of others is by far the least expensive and the least painful way to gain, vicariously, the experience that otherwise comes only from extended exposure to the risks and vagaries of the marketplace. There have been precious few books or resources made available prior to publication of this book which specifically deal with losing periods or experiences, which can give the trader the benefit of learning from the losing periods of others. Most of the other "interview" types of books deal with the successful experiences, the methodology, or the background of the participants, but do not deal specifically with situations of the type described in this book. And, it is just human nature that most folks tend to tell you about their good luck and their trading successes, and sweep the bad and the losing experiences "under the rug."

Art Collins is to be commended for his foresight in coming up with the idea for this book, and for his hard work and diligent effort in "making it happen." He speaks from the standpoint of one who has "been there" himself. His first book, *Market Rap: The Odyssey of a Still Struggling Commodity Trader* (also published by *Traders Press*) is in itself a valuable contribution and insight into the difficulties involved in becoming a successful trader, and is also highly recommended.

It is a privilege and an honor to be associated with the publication of this fine book. All of us at Traders Press wish to express our appreciation to those herein who gave so generously of their time so the rest of us can benefit from what they have experienced and learned before. Many of them are personal friends and acquaintances who I have known for many years, and I am especially pleased to have them included in this book. It is my hope that this book will benefit you, the trader, and that it will make your journey to success in trading an easier and less painful experience.

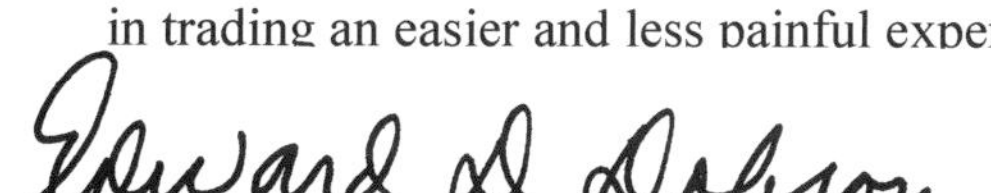

Edward D. Dobson, President
*Traders Press, Inc.*®
Greenville, SC

December 1, 2001

# *Acknowledgments*

I want to thank my friend, Larry Zajac, who did the fine cover art of this book. He also, as usual, offered support and feedback, editorial and otherwise, in a frank, no B.S. way that I can always trust.

Thanks to my parents, Norman and Norma (yes, really), who have hung with me even through their occasional concerns and reservations.

To my publisher, Ed Dobson: It's a near-impenetrable wall standing in the way of a first published work. For whatever moved him to take that initial chance (as well as this second one), I'll always be grateful.

Thanks to my friend and partner, Mark LaSarre, for his invaluable contribution toward making our financial dream a reality.

To the late Bruce Babcock, who, four years ago, encouraged me to launch my investment writing career.

To Howard Malman, for giving me my first proprietary trading opportunity.

To Adrienne Laris Toghraie, who offered insight and encouragement regarding publication and promotion.

To Bruce Williams, Jack Kotz, John Baca, Tom Murray and Neal Weintraub, for the special role they played in procuring contacts for this project.

To Ruth Barrons Roosevelt, for taking the time to write the foreword.

And to all of my 35 subjects, who were forthright, painfully honest at times, informative, colorful and fun. Hope I done 'em all proud.

# *Preface*

Never let it be said that I can dish it out while not being able to take it.

My personal loss stories could fill a book. But come to think of it, I already wrote it—*Market Rap: The Odyssey of a Still-Struggling Commodity Trader*. I laid myself bare in that one, to the point where a few of my acquaintances started squinting at me like they were looking through one of those pinprick solar eclipse devices.

Since writing it, I've had a few more misadventures, including one (detailed in the next section) that resulted from so many things going simultaneously wrong, it almost defies belief. But it's true, I assure you, as are so many other "at-the-edge" stories within these pages. If you trade long enough, you too will eventually have anecdotes in the realm of the surreal.

The book you're holding contains stories by top echelon traders—people who, through unique talents, have risen significantly above the usual trading fray. It is a chronicle of anomalies—unusually bad events that occurred in otherwise skillfully engineered, triumphant trading careers.

They are important tales. If losses are universal—and whoever trades inevitably encounters them—then it's instructive to know how the best among us coped. Why did the reversals occur? To what frailties did the wizards succumb? How did they resolve their situations? How did they react to them emotionally? What lasting impact resulted? What did the traders learn and how did their trading styles change?

In what ways were they like you and I? (Or different)?

Traders are a unique breed. It takes a healthy ego to be able to say, "I am going up against nothing but markets—I don't need to work with anyone, I can do it alone. Forget hierarchies; forget training manuals, seminars... Forget steady paychecks...."

To paraphrase Mark Cook, one of my interviewees, they evoke an aura of "grandeur"—they aren't as a rule, "self deprecating." One doesn't easily extract trading foibles from people who embody such exactitude, decision-making aptitude, calculated risk taking, courage—and ego.

So not surprisingly, I encountered some resistance in the course of this project. It was rewarding, even exhilarating, but no cakewalk. Some people said no. Some said yes and had second thoughts. I had maybe two or three weeks of my life squandered by traders who weren't where they said they'd be for interviews. Some freaked the second I turned on the tape recorder. Some were obviously less than forthright to the point where they wasted my time, as well as, I assume, their own.

The theme of *Kryptonite* was actually conceived by my publisher, Edward Dobson. I think he selected me largely because I was inexperienced enough not to know what to fear. But I'm not bitching. This was truly one of the standout experiences of my life.

There wasn't a field I didn't attempt to mine. The Chicago pits provided a great variety of stories. Other subjects, from every corner of the country, contributed via phone interviews. Some are renowned celebrities; others are rich, but relatively obscure and jealously protective of their privacy.

My trading friends weren't immune from my hounding. Some shocked me with events I'd had no idea occurred. As for others...well, I'm sure it's a coincidence that their phone numbers changed. (Kidding). I'm no longer, as one of my friends put it, "one of the paparazzi." (Not at the moment anyway).

Despite the occasional speed bump, however, *Kryptonite* was, for the most part, an endeavor of remarkably smooth sailing. The accessibility and candor were beyond anything I'd anticipated. I'd get an amazing story that I figured would be a standout, and then three more of comparable worth would immediately follow.

The thirty-five subjects within were gracious and helpful. They were vital in steering me toward other traders. I owe them, plus a few other trading associates, a huge debt of gratitude.

Someone may well point out that I too often seem excessively sympathetic or apologetic for my interviewees, like the young rock writer in "Almost Famous." Watta groupie. While I'm hoping I never lost my objectivity, I'll freely admit, I do love traders. Like no one else, they embody what was once a more prevalent entrepreneurial, creative pioneer spirit in this society.

The market arena survives as an ultimate proving ground—a place of self-assessment and self-discovery unlike any other. In so many ways, trading is an allegory for life. So much of what can be experienced in the world at large can be distilled down into those magical octagonal pits or computerized trading screens.

I spent years working in a business in which I didn't belong, stealing all the time off I could in order to eventually become a trader. I remember at the time being forced to deal with trader mirror-image counterparts, bankers, and loan officers. (I was the finance manager in an auto dealership). Such officials wouldn't commit to extending money until every safety net imaginable was in perfect place for them. Personally, they tended to be as stodgy and closed-off as the traders were wide-open and life affirming.

There were exceptions, of course, (including some good drinking companions), but as a rule, I didn't relate to the money-lenders. I don't like that play-it-safe-by-the-book world. Locking in your five percent may be prudent—but shooting for your two hundred percent will make you alive. Or contribute to an early death. That's the rub of the trading world—you can never be sure of tomorrow.

On the other hand, that's part of the adventure.

# Art Collins
# A PERSONAL FIASCO

*Remember those Rube Goldberg cartoons? They depicted weird, convoluted chain reactions involving bathtubs and birdcages and windmills—all working together to make something simple happen, such as blowing out a candle. Something was always falling off a ledge onto one end of a seesaw, which would catapult something into something else, and before you knew it, you'd have a rocket launch that started from a mouse stealing a piece of cheese.*

*That encapsulates my latest market disaster story. It was a comedy of errors befitting Shakespeare, or perhaps "The Beverly Hillbillies." Had any one of the roughly half-dozen miscues not occurred, my partner, Nick Bressner**, and I would not have suffered our unscheduled $15,000 loss.*

*Unlike most market disaster stories I encountered, ours didn't occur at the tail end of a successful account run up. Actually, it immediately followed another mistake—one that had also made a $15,000 difference.*

*We're system traders. Nothing we do is judgmental; it's all a result of what we've discovered in historical research. Like other system traders, our objective is to remove the twin human frailties of fear and greed. We have proscribed rules for everything; how and why we initiate, when we take profits, and where we place our stop losses. We never have to ask each other, "What do you think? What do we do now?"*

---

***Fictitious name.*

*Until the unforeseen occurs. No matter how rigid your guidelines, sooner or later you're going to say, "buy" when you meant, "sell" over the phone, or you're going to strike a wrong key.*

*An anxiety peculiar to system traders is they can always torment themselves over what they were supposed to do, what they left on the table, etc. There's no problem reconstructing theoretically correct system plays. The right path is always out there in plain view. Some system advocates claim they've suffered more over missed winning trade opportunities than over actual monetary losses.*

*Leading into our complicated mishap, Nick Bressner and I were still smarting over the $15,000 extra we were supposed to have earned a week earlier. As the guy managing the trades, I knew I couldn't afford any more screw-ups. Even harmonious partnerships like ours have their breaking points.*

*In November 2000, Nick and I decided to start entering our orders online. The system we were using wasn't the purely electronic Globex. We didn't have direct access to bids and offers, but rather, our orders would be routed into the trading pit. It was therefore sort of a halfway measure between the old outcry system and the new online one, and there was a time delay between striking the entry key and receiving confirmation.*

*We had learned in recent days that our setup was lacking some functions. We couldn't, for example, put up MOC (market on close) orders in the e-mini S&Ps.*

*I was supposed to buy two full-sized S&Ps on the close. We were short one, and a reverse-momentum close-only system was telling us it was time to flip to the other side. I wasn't sure whether the e-mini MOC restriction also applied to the full contracts, and since I only had seconds left to get the order up, I decided to go with a market order, trying to time it as close as possible to the approximate MOC time frame.*

*I waited for confirmation. The market closed, and I waited some more. Five minutes after the close, I nervously phoned my online rep, Meredith. "Let me call the pit," she said.*

*I re-dialed Nick—again, after our prior $15,000 mishap, I wanted him prepared for every development—no surprises. As I was talking to him, Meredith clicked into my call waiting and told me that the order was received too late to fill. I informed Nick. He and I then decided that I shouldn't have any trouble getting filled on the Globex session, due to start in 25 minutes.*

*This set the stage for the following:*

1. As the now-dead order continues to sit in our "working orders" screen, I put up a market order to buy two at the opening of the after-hours session.

2. I do so by hitting the "electronic session" option—my choice is either that or "normal hours."

3. Unbeknownst to me, the electronic accommodation isn't available at all. I'd later learn that during certain times of the day, some markets simply don't lend themselves to online....you have to phone things in the old fashioned way. For five or ten more minutes, I wait while no confirmation comes through.

4. Since I have no idea that my service is so inept, I figure that, for some reason, it wants me to stipulate "normal hours." I cancel-replace the order, correctly deducing that there would be no danger of a double-fill. Either the original electronic glitch would be resolved and the new order would be rejected, or the new order would replace the old one—in either case, one fill.

5. Unfortunately, I had made another error. All day long, I had been trading not just the partnership, but my personal account as well. Just prior to putting up the order, I had flipped to my own screen to check out some e-mini positions...and failed to go back. Our partnership order was now sitting in my personal account.

6. While all this is going on, the market suddenly begins lurching. The S&Ps are now two points higher than the regular-session closing price at which I was supposed to have bought them. Please Lord...I can't handle another mistake. Meanwhile...

7. For the second time of the day, I'm still waiting for a fill that doesn't materialize. With panic welling, I call Meredith. Nick, in one of the most inopportune moments in history, than clicks into my call waiting. My dogs are barking incessantly at some mope who dared walk across our back yard. No fill—rocketing market—pandemonium.

8. In a disastrous attempt at division of labor, I tell Nick that I'll handle our new entry order with Meredith, and he should cancel our existing one. (Anyone with a password has screen access). I'm of course, referring to the second online after-hours order. The first day session one is completely out of my thoughts—it is, after all, dead—no threat.

9. Nick, though, can't see the order I'm talking about—it's in my personal account. He cancels the only accessible one—the dead one that was placed during the normal session. "Did you do it?" "Yes I did"—in both our minds, Mission Accomplished.

MEANWHILE—
10. The market dips back down, and Meredith fills us at our desired price. At the same time, a live order, stipulating "normal hours" sits in my account like a ticking time bomb. It will detonate unseen at 8:30 a.m. the next morning, Friday—the start of the normal open outcry session.

11. I'm happy with my daily and weekly personal trading results. I therefore vow not to trade my own account the next day. Historically, Fridays have a way of getting more out of control than any other, (for me, anyway), which may have something to do with trader masochism. Screw up, and you have the whole weekend to flagellate yourself.

And, as I detailed in my last book, *Market Rap*, system trading is the only thing that works for me anyhow. My personal account activity has been, at best, a mere pressure-release plaything indulgence. Since 1997, our partnership has been responsible for about 98 percent of my trading activity, and 100 percent of my profits.

No personal Friday moves—I've declared it Law, and I'm A Prudent Guy.

12. Friday morning, both accounts show expected positions, equity and trade activity. The Bomb is not documented—it is just now going off in some other far-off real time horizon.

Throughout the day, I refer to my partnership's "working" and "filled," order screens. I don't monitor my individual one. My statement was in order, and I'm not trading there today.

13. Saturday morning, I finally see the two S&P longs assigned to me. The statement had me buying on the opening—the ensuing high of the day. At present, the con-tracts represent a $12,000 loss.

I still can't account for them. I can now see that they match Friday's open, but as I keep telling myself over and over, I hadn't done anything that day. Thursday was my last involvement with my own account, but my price was under that day's low. And besides—all were accounted for.

14. I couldn't see how my bases weren't covered, but I was getting uneasy anyway. As I'd learned already, electronic postings are seldom erroneous. Intent has nothing to do with accountability—it's all in your actual key strokes. In cyberspace trading, what you click is both cut-and-dried, and readily traceable.

15. So I drive my poor wife, Pat, crazy all weekend—I'm not one to stoically suffer. I also call Nick for reassurance. "What do you think?" "I don't know Artie, what could it be?" "I don't know—probably nothing." I doubtthat at this point Nick was considering he might have a personal stake in the mess.

16. Monday morning, after a couple hours of still being in the dark, I'm assured that the orders were placed on my terminal at such-and-such time of day.

Blah blah. I'm nailed as though my DNA were all over the room.

17. An hour later, I have the events reconstructed. TO RECAP—An initial order was placed and not filled. My partner, who mistook it for the second live one I had put up, eventually canceled it. But he couldn't have gotten to that one because it was mistakenly sitting in my personal account. Also, because it was stipulated as a "normal hours" order, it wasn't filled until the next morning on the open. Because the trade occurred too late to show up in the statement, and because no one was expecting it, it wasn't detected until a day after that, after it had already hemorrhaged $12,000.

And then the market opened another $3,000 against us.

The clearing personnel immediately filled us, locking in our second $15,000 losing mistake within a week.

Nick is an honorable guy. He immediately told me to move the contracts into the partnership before I could even ask him.

The moral implications however, haunt me to this day. On the one hand, yes, it was system-linked—I clearly wouldn't have done anything without partnership-related mandates. Still, I can't justify my own account playing a part in my "too-harried-to-respond" scenario. Nick is powerless as I handle his money—he deserves better.

One other thing bothered me as well. I tried to imagine a flip side event—two contracts in my account representing a sudden windfall. Even forgetting good or bad intentions—where would my innocent inclinations have led? If no one, including Nick, were desperate to solve the mystery—how far would I have persevered to uncover it? Pat's assurance aside—"you've always tried to protect your partner"—the two scenarios seemed disturbingly incongruous.

Since accountability is so clear-cut in system trading, the lessons we learned weren't much beyond the "tighten everything up—double-check everything" variety. I'm reasonably sure I'll never again confuse trading accounts—perhaps the worst of the series of bad steps. Referring to order numbers would have eliminated confusion over what trades we were talking about. If Nick couldn't find Order 112, I would have surely traced it back to my own account in time to avert disaster.

It always helps to know your playing field though—don't wait until the world is spinning out of control before you're consulting with your own version of Meredith. Know exactly what orders you can execute, and all the logistics of online, or whatever trading arena. Know them in the quiet solitude of your pre-market hour planning stages.

All simple enough. I'm sure as time goes on, we'll implement evermore safeguards—probably as a result of having learned more lessons the hard way. There will always be new hurdles, though—the markets won't ever stop being formidable, daunting...and occasionally maddening. Few participants will ever completely eradicate their personal kryptonite—not even the supertraders among us.

***On to their stories....***

~

*Bill Beach*

# Chapter 1

## Bill Beach

### "I WAS OUT 45 TICKS BY THE TIME I PUKED THEM."

*Bill Beach's introduction to the Chicago Board of Trade is a story that may live long in the annals of trading legend. It certainly demonstrates how weird fate can be.*

*After recounting it, Bill, with unusual candor, then shared his yearly earning results, and my mind was blown even further.*

*Bill Beach was obviously destined to be a successful trader, but I doubt many people would have bet on him during his inauspicious beginnings. He was a decidedly unworldly Oklahoma resident, fresh out of college without a clue as to where life would take him. A cattle rancher-friend basically told him, go east, young man, find your fortune at the Chicago exchanges.*

*"I didn't know what Chicago looked like," said Bill. "I'd never been on a plane before."*

*He cashed $1,500 in bonds that his grandparents had given him. Upon landing, he discovered that the big city wasn't exactly waiting for him with open arms. He couldn't get hired at the exchanges or anywhere else.*

*He frequented the visitor's gallery at the Chicago Board of Trade, watching traders in action. It was then and there he decided he'd someday own a yellow badge (full membership).*

*He was down to his last $200 and contemplating a return to Oklahoma when, one night in a bar, he began conversing with the sister of a friend who—as fate would have it—worked at the Board. Oh, you were hoping to be a trader, she said, well come on down to the Board, I'll get you a job! She explained apologetically that it would only be for $150 a week. Bill said "Sold!" and the next thing he knew, he was hired by a clearing firm to be a personal runner for options trader David Show.*

*"She gave me a great buildup," laughed Bill. "She told him she knew me since kindergarten!"*

*The stock market crash of 1987 put Bill's company out of business. From there, he got hired to do clerical work for crush and silver speculator, Milt Robinson. Milt was making proprietary financial arrangements with several traders, and Bill eventually asked if he too could get such a deal. His boss rather unenthusiastically agreed.*

*Bill began his trading career in 1989, arbing gold and silver between the New York and Chicago markets. He was also trading back month bond spreads during the then-existing evening pit session.*

*Within five months of his entry, the Board's metals markets pretty much dried up, so Bill moved to the muni bond pit. He had already determined that spreading** was his forte—he had an innate sense of when various contracts were out of line. He began working the munis against both 30-year bonds and 10-year notes, while continuing his evening session activity.*

---

***A spreader simultaneously buys, or goes long one contract while selling, or going short another. All other things being equal, the trader will profit if the side he is long rises more than, or drops less than his short side. Spreaders, therefore, are not concerned with overall market direction, but rather, the relative movement between different contracts.*

He never lost the conviction, however, that something positive was going to eventually give somewhere. "I didn't think it was going to carry me out."

Throughout Bill's wild upward ride and beyond, he maintained his usual conservative life-style. True, he bought the seat, and purchased a house just after getting married in 1995, but, as he explained, "I didn't own any furniture, and I didn't own a car. The house I bought was a good deal, just a trader kind of a thing to do. I got the edge on it."

So he could, in effect, sit tight through his ordeal and wait for the thaw to return, which it did in November. Going into the month, he was down $150,000, having clawed his way back from his June nadir. When the year was over, he was up $250,000. He was so buoyed by the feat of having so turned a corner that the momentum propelled him into another seven-figure profit in 1997. Unfortunately, the close of that year also brought more adversity—Bill was diagnosed with Type One diabetes.

"Your emotional health determines how you trade," said Bill. It was another observation many sources would subsequently affirm.

He came to regard 1998 as a year of "survival mode," for both him and his wife, Debbie. It was his first and, to-date, only net loser; minus $500,000.

The diagnosis was "pretty devastating," Bill admitted.

His condition also created some logistical problems relative to his trading. Prior to learning about it, Bill would never take a break from the pit. Suddenly, he was forced to contend with eating and taking insulin at strictly regimented times. He'd leave, come back, and find that his focus was gone.

"I was probably averaging 70 percent losses on the trades when I'd first return," he estimated.

He thinks his trading life might have impacted his health as much as the reverse was true. His big earning years were certainly satisfying, but Bill regards them as having been emotionally taxing as well.

"I am very much a person who internalizes stress," he said. "I always had a 'never-let -'em-see-you-sweat' kind of attitude." Because diabetes is an autoimmune disorder, Bill suspects his environment may have contributed to its onset.

Nevertheless, throughout his struggles, he remained determined to confront his illness head-on. He followed his regimen so religiously that his doctor pronounced him the best diabetic patient she'd ever had in her practice.

Bill conceded that he's more successful trading down markets than up ones, which might also have factored into his 98 debit. The financials were rallying sharply in response to the crashing Nikkei market and the monetary crisis among the Pacific rim nations. He was trading bigger than ever, but unfortunately not in the right way at the right times.

In 1999, he regained his footing as another down market hit. "I came in still a little shell-shocked, but a little more cautious."

Probably what aided his outlook more than anything was the yearly changeover. "December 31st may be just a date," he observed, "but it symbolizes a lot."

He can now trade around his enforced absences from the pit. He's back to achieving returns well into the six figures and beyond, and has modified his life in ways extending beyond his diabetes.

He is in the acceptance stage of the grief process that accompanies chronic illness. He's less likely to let his perfectionism undermine him.

"I can accept my feelings and my frailties," he said. The fact that he's less fanatical now about following his health regimen probably does him more good than harm—he can occasionally splurge on what he craves without feeling he's undermined his entire treatment.

He's better learning how to enjoy life. He doesn't feel he has to handle everything flawlessly. In a giant step for him, he took off 85 trading days in 1999. (The perfectionist in him may have performed the tally, but...progress isn't always instantaneous).

In March 2000, the muni volume dropped to unsustainable levels, so Bill moved to the just-introduced 10-year agency bonds. Considering the fact he'd been standing in the same pit for over a decade, it was an adjustment. He lost $250,000 his first month, but typically, reclaimed it and then some two months later. He realized another solid six figure gain by year's end.

With obvious good reason, Bill has an unshakable faith in himself. Even in his darkest hours, he doesn't recall a time when he got down in a clinical sense.

"Depressed? No, I don't think so," he said. "I'm a fairly upbeat, optimistic person."

*Steve Miller*

# Chapter 2

## Steve L. Miller

### "I remember the day I had $5600 in my account. This was down from well over a million dollars."

*In 1983, Steven L. Miller became one of the original screen trading pioneers. The concept was not yet widely familiar, computerized charts were still in the Stone Age and there were no organized after-hours online markets. Nobody was anticipating that open outcry would be jeopardized within a couple of decades.*

*The floor was still King, and Steve had enjoyed many successful years in the various pits of Chicago exchanges. He was one of the original market makers in the Chicago Board Options Exchange's OEX market, although atypically, he could often be found standing outside the pit monitoring his many holdings.*

*"I was spending a lot of time looking at the Quotron," he said. "I traded a lot of different stocks at once. Just based on my style, I was naturally pulled out of the pit."*

*Steve arrived on the CBOE floor in 1974. He owned a menswear business at the time. One of his partner's sons started working at the CBOE, which got the partner-father interested enough to buy a seat. Steve followed suit, and soon the clothing business was on the selling block.*

*For nearly ten years, Steve traded the OEX, Ford and IBM options, as well as in nearly every other pit on the CBOE floor. In 1981, he further expanded his market universe by purchasing a Chicago Board of Trade seat. He used it to trade soybeans, 30-year bonds and bond options. Around that time, he also began his long-term involvement with the Mercantile Exchange's S&P futures contract. To expedite his performance, he sent his personal team of brokers into the pit.*

*After making the move to his upstairs screens, he spent three years publishing the SLM Technical Trading Advisory letter starting in 1994. SLM was his floor acronym as well as an abbreviation of the nickname he would later acquire—"Slim."*

*"It was generally a life-stealer," he said of his newsletter venture. "It took from three or four in the morning until six at night every day to get this letter produced. So although I had aspired to do that, I found out that I hated it."*

*Throughout his 26-year career, Steve has frequently mentored other traders. His coaching focuses on the psychological aspects of the business, plus cyclical and technical characteristics of the financial markets.*

*Aside from that, he was back to personal full-time trading, much to his relief. In 1997, he moved into individual stocks. One year later, he was hired by Peregrine Financial Group Inc. to be the senior trader. He managed large-scale accounts, ($200,000 minimum). Recently, he has scaled back his commitment in order to focus on the launching of a hedge fund.*

*He still trades for himself, but is careful to keep his managed universe separate from his personal one. He trades only financial futures, stock index futures and options for his firm, and individual equities for his own account.*

---

Many of us might gladly assume the career trajectory of Steven L. Miller, even considering his nightmare reversals and long periods of despair. His knack for wealth accumulation is certainly enviable.

But there had once been a dark side to Steve Miller as well, and he's unusually forthright in disclosing it.

"The amount of money I made was my identity," he said. "Throughout my career, after taking a big loss, I'd go through a regrouping period where I'd have to pull it in, examine what's real in my life, and find a base that meant something beyond the money. I'd always have to go back to square one."

His trading life became one of wild swings. He'd be on top of the world as his equity exploded. Then as it started to evaporate, he would enter a vicious cycle in which he'd get despondent, panic, and then make his losses worse.

His personal soul-searching wasn't turning up much. Eventually, four different therapists and social workers would similarly come up short. Relief and clarity wouldn't result until after he was forced to endure several major emotional roller coaster rides. The first occurred in 1978.

"I had been successful in 1975 and '76, when I was twenty-five and twenty-six years old," he said. "I had made $250,000 and $300,000 each year. 1977 was kind of flat for me.

"In the spring of '78, I had anticipated that there was going to be a large (equities) rally. I'd made some money up to that point in the year, so I bought two thousand options contracts all over the CBOE floor. All calls."

He was ultimately right about the rally, but unfortunately, about two weeks too early. The market broke sharply, forcing him to liquidate with a $250,000 loss. He was suddenly faced with the trader anathema of being down on the year. Had he been able to hold on for another month, his position would have been worth three million.

"I was married five years at the time. My wife endured many difficult emotional swings over my career. That was a tough one.

"Once the big rally started and I started trading well again, I went from being down about $50,000 on the year to up about $600,000 by September."

Steve then decided that the market was going to fall, and positioned himself short in the equities. This time, he was dead-on.

"Coming into November first, I was up a million-four for the year. That particular move ended with what still stands as my biggest day ever; $321,000."

He didn't know it at the time, but that first day in November would represent a personal pinnacle for him that would stand for a gut-wrenching long period while his equity would drop to unimaginable depths.

"The next day, President Carter raised interest rates a full point and I lost $341,000. So my best and worst days were back-to-back. I took off for the year after that day, and I have never worked a full December since."

He still ended up earning 1.1 million for the year, which, understandably, gave him considerable satisfaction. Unfortunately, it wouldn't last long.

"By June of 1980, I was broke. I remember the day that I had $5,600 in my trading account. This was down from well over a million dollars."

His fortunes finally turned on what might suggest something out of "The Twilight Zone." First, he responded to an eerie premonition.

"I felt a weird chill come over my body," said Steve. "It was very odd and directed me into the Storage Technology pit with a confidence not commensurate with my financial situation.

"That afternoon, I get a call from my mother who was at my house. She says, 'I just threw salt all over the house to get rid of the evil spirits.' I didn't believe in any of that, but that's what she did."

Steve was holding a rather complicated options strategy in Storage Technology that suddenly paid off. He had a reverse conversion on, meaning he was long calls, short puts, and short the underlying equities. That day, he made $30,000, which launched him on a relentless march back to his triumphant levels.

"I don't know if it had anything to do with the salt," he laughed.

Steve then enjoyed some more golden years in 1983-85.

"I practically made $100,000 a month every month without a break, including a $400,000 month. I earned roughly three million dollars during that period.

"I built an 11,000 square foot house. I owned two Rolls Royce's. I did everything I could to create this giant structure that portrayed an identity that was...valueless."

In December 1985, while vacationing in Florida, Steve purchased his second Rolls—a $94,500 Cornish convertible. He earned that exact amount on the first trading day of 1986, the very day it was delivered to his house. With his single session windfall, he paid off his purchase in full.

A few days later, the Challenger space shuttle exploded and the stock market broke. Moves emanating out of such sudden surprises often don't sustain. The market will roil, but tend to snap back in slingshot-like fashion.

Unfortunately, Steve was convinced that this time, the downmove was legitimate, so he sold into the ensuing rally. He had started the day at, what was to date, the peak of his trading career. By the close, he was $50,000 off his pinnacle.

"I spent the next six or seven years chasing that money," he recalled. "I got divorced. I had to sell the house. For many many years, I never recovered my trading stride."

By 1994, he was on the sidelines. He opened a few mall kiosks during the Christmas holidays, and was selling ties and belts.

Then a trader friend urged him to go on a weekend retreat with a chapter of the New Warriors. The group was founded by three men in Milwaukee during the mid-eighties, and inspired by poet Robert Bly, who is also famous for the men's manifesto **Iron John**. Its goal is to help men identify and cope with "the wounds of their lives." Twenty thousand participants have since done the training.

Steve was initially reluctant. "I don't like being involved in groups. I handle things on my own. What good could this do me?"

Besides, he didn't have the necessary $600 fee. His friend told him "you're going, this is the date, and it's paid for."

"Being that I was in incredible pain and had no direction, I said 'OK, I'll go.' It turned out to be the most profound thing that could have ever happened in my life."

He finally had answers regarding his self-destructiveness. He has since been involved with the group on a weekly basis. He acts as facilitator—one who follows up with members after they've received initial training.

"I discovered a different way of living—of communicating. I've since remarried and have a great relationship with my wife, Gail, who has also done this type of work in the women's version, 'Woman Within'."

He is now thriving in the markets in a much more consistent fashion. He gave a recent example of how he stayed on top of a stressful situation in a way he admitted would have been previously impossible.

"I had anticipated a market decline the day (Federal Reserve Board Chairman Alan) Greenspan surprised it with a half point rate cut. I lost $280,000 in less than 180 seconds. It was just a bad day. I wouldn't measure myself by it, but I decided that the markets were going to be a little more difficult. So three days after the event, after I had recovered half my loss, I took a week off. I rested, re-grounded myself, came back, and was back on track."

No chasing the market this time; no craziness. The incident was an isolated event, not an overall indictment of Steve Miller. Steve now understood that, and realized he had nothing to prove.

"It's made a huge difference in my life because now, I don't measure myself by how much I make every day trading. In the past, I needed to chase the money so I could feel good about myself."

A lay-pop psychologist might be tempted to paint Steve's history with a broad "compulsive personality" brush. When he was chasing his money, for example, he seemed to fit the problem gambler profile. Was it beyond his control? Did he also have trouble with, for example, controlled substances?

"No, I didn't really," he said. "I didn't drink. I didn't do drugs. I quit smoking in '82. I didn't really have vices.

"My addiction was the need to make money. When I was doing well, I felt great and all the underlying real pain in my life was numbed. The underlying pain was a sense of unworthiness that only super-achieving could cover.

"Money was my drug. Now, I feel good about myself for every other reason."

~

*Walter Bressert*

# CHAPTER 3

# WALTER BRESSERT

## "...AND THEN I'D HAVE THE 'WALK-ON-WATER' COMPLEX..."

*Walter Bressert is reputed to be the first person to base an advisory service on the field of market cycle analysis. Since the late 1960s, he has provided his subscribers with a comprehensive investment picture that combines oscillators, Fibonacci numbers and other technical indicators with cyclical timing. His numerous publication credits include the* HAL Commodity Cycles *and* CycleWatch *newsletters, as well as his 1991 book,* ***The Power of Oscillator/Cycle Combinations.*** *He has also written for* The Wall Street Journal, Barron's, Futures Magazine, *and* The Commodity Research Bureau Yearbook. *He currently edits and publishes* MarketWatch, *a daily journal providing cycle-based recommendations in stock indexes, bonds and various futures.*

*Walter invented Timing Bands, a tool that reflects the tendency cycles have to expand and contract. He developed ProfitTrader software which, like the rest of his work, provides subscribers with the means of making their own market decisions based on his studies.*

*One of the most recognized speakers at industry workshops and seminars, Walter is cited by several industry people, including mechanical system expert Charlie Wright, as a major influence.*

*Walter also trades for his own account. Many contracts.*

In the course of writing this book, I have come across a variety of circumstances leading to significant losses. Walter Bressert was the first to attribute losing a million dollars to sheer neglect.

"The hog market stands out as the dumbest loss I ever took," said Walter, "because I simply closed my eyes and wished it to go away."

He had amassed several million dollars in the wild silver and soybean markets of the seventies and early eighties. He did it consistently and easily enough that, as frequently happens, he began to feel "bulletproof." His normally analytical trading approach was suddenly out the window.

"As a matter of fact, I was in the Bahamas for a week, doing a seminar. I would call up every now and then and check, and every time, it had gotten a little worse. I figured it was going to finally turn around and go my way. I had made so much money that I just figured it had to do what I wanted it to do."

Walter's methodology was to enter a market just off a cycle extreme, and then build what he termed a "campaign" upon it. He would continue to add to his position, occasionally taking some off to capitalize on short term cycle turning points, but overall, steadily increasing his position as the market advanced.

As other big traders have recounted, success sometimes involves sitting through open ongoing losses, only to ultimately close them out at more advantageous levels. Walter again anticipated his customary retracement which, this time, never occurred. He was finally forced to say "uncle;" a million dollars lighter.

Speculators are all prone to the same foibles of course, which Walter addresses in his "The 12 Cardinal Mistakes" trading guide. He'd obviously ignored #3, "failure to use protective stop/loss orders," #4, "taking small profits and letting your losses run" and #5, "overstaying your position."

"What I find among those I teach," said Walter, "is, one, they want to be right. Two, they don't want to take a loss." He makes no bones about the fact that he had persistently been in that company.

His other chronic shortcoming was related to his money-amassing campaigns. He would simply not recognize when it was time to stop adding, and time to scale back or take profits. The higher his account soared, the more prone he became to euphoria and greed.

"My trading history is one of spectacular profits, and then big losses off of the (equity) highs. I would get my account up substantially, and then I'd have the 'walk-on-water' complex that you tend to get. Total overconfidence"

He would then give back significant money—sometimes enough to more than erase his entire windfall. He recounted one story of how his whole campaign had been one of astonishing accuracy, right down to a projected ultimate high. He was long through it all, but as the target high approached, he inexplicably decided that there was more upside left. At a time when he should have been bailing entirely, he actually added to his position. Unfortunately, his original profit projection provcd all-to-accurate, and the resulting collapse forced him to exit in the red.

Walter also lost $1,000,000 in the pork belly market; not once, but twice. He regards at least one of the episodes as "probably the epitome of every possible mistake a human being could make.

"I didn't know what I was doing. I had just made several million in the silver market—I had a good handle on the cycles. I knew to hold on as silver took off. I added on regressively as the cycles bottomed.

"I had this huge run, and I started looking around for what I was going to trade next. Bellies had a great cycle."

As it turns out, however, Walter typically had more in his trading arsenal than mere technical indicators. He understood the pit logistics that were necessary to accommodate his large presence. By his own admission, he'd had a lot of help from floor brokers. "They'd keep me from destroying myself." He knew how much the market could handle before disruptions would occur.

His approach to bellies, however, involved "just throwing contracts" at it.

"There is a week on the charts that just reflects me. I don't think you can find another spot on historical belly charts that looks like it.

"I didn't realize how the floor operated. Despite all my years of trading, I was kind of naive, I suppose."

He initially entered an order to buy 100 contracts, which due to the contract's lack of liquidity, was filled limit up. He decided to get out, and again, not being cognizant of his personal affect on the market, was forced to exit his position at limit down. At the time, 400 points or $800 per contract separated the two daily allowable price extremes. After that, he continued to fight the market, buying highs, selling lows, and sometimes getting caught the wrong way in limit positions. To say the least, his usual bean-silver approach was not working here.

"To make a long story short," said Walter, "I took it limit up, limit down, limit up, limit down, limit up, limit down, and I kept going like that, and I'd get stuck" (in an adverse limit position).

He finally took his Mega-Loss. The broker handling his orders was later fined for allowing Walter to trade "well beyond" the trading limits. Because there had been no such restraints in the metals, Walter had assumed that all futures markets were as wide-open.

In some ways, Walter Bressert seems an almost contradictory composite. Both his scientific and intuitive approach are on a par with the most celebrated wizards. The fact that he can effectively combine the two is unusual—mechanical proponents tend to see their trading arenas in all-or-nothing terms.

Walter has enjoyed upper-echelon-level success, and yet, his missteps have been equally colossal. Despite what he intellectually knows to be true about trading, he confessed to having been at the extreme end of market-related emotional turmoil. He alluded to depression-like bouts—"going into the closet" as he termed it.

"For two to four weeks, I was incapable of doing anything. I wasn't able to trade, I wasn't able to function with my family. I was living in a dark cloud."

His phenomenal success ironically most contributed to his carelessness; large trading losses didn't initially impact him because immediately prior, there had been such a huge, fortifying monetary cushion. That proved to be little comfort, however, in later times of reflection and self-recrimination.

Walter would routinely pull himself out of the depths within three or four weeks of an episode. His self-induced therapy would be the resumption of work.

"I'd start looking at my charts again. That's my way to relax. I'd get into my cycles, I'd see something coming up, and the juices would again start flowing."

Still, he was in a recurring pattern of running vast sums up and down, and having his emotions swing as widely. In 1985, he knew he was becoming overwhelmed. He began a five year hiatus from most of his trading, lecturing, and travel-related career activities.

"I had burnt myself out," he admitted. "When I analyzed what the problem had been, I realized it was constant stress and judgments. With that came the whole emotional trip—feeling remorse, feeling jubilation...."

So Walter made some modifications. He altered his trading time frame to be more intra-day oriented; his campaigns became built around cycles on a seven minute bar chart. He also added mechanical entry signals to his intuitive techniques. The adjustment converted most of his hardest decisions into automatic signals. Within a couple years, he had reclaimed his rhythm, and was now trading in a way more conducive to his personal serenity.

The emotionless entries don't determine trend direction, but do tend to occur at or near cycle turning points. With this knowledge, Walter purportedly can identify bottoms with from 70% to 90% accuracy—tops from 65% to 80%, depending on the type of signal. This establishes a crucial setup which treats an existing high or low as an area that is likely to hold. Most people, merely engaging in top and bottom picking, have a harder time quantifying their risk.

"If it's a bottom, it's going to go up after it's a bottom," said Walter. "You use momentum to confirm it. Once you know you have a good solid bottom, you've got a place for a good solid stop." (Just beneath it).

"Then you're in control."

The control doesn't stop with markets. As affirmed by many other top individuals, general balance in life is crucial to successful trading. Walter doesn't agonize over market decisions any more. He exercises religiously, does yoga and meditates. And of course, he continues to write and lecture and therapeutically pore over his data....living the way he knows he must.

"If you're not balanced in this game," observed Walter, "you grow old quickly."

*Tony Saliba*

## Chapter 4

# Tony Saliba

## "I GRABBED A BASEBALL BAT, AND WAS A HAIR'S-BREADTH AWAY FROM BLOODYING HIS SKULL."

*Ask for stock option trading legends and Tony Saliba will likely be one of the first names mentioned. Immortalized in Jack Schwager's* ***Market Wizards****, Tony has been a giant Chicago Board Options Exchange presence almost since the beginning of his two-decade-plus career. He entered the brokerage business directly out of college. A year and a half later, he was clerking on the CBOE floor. Within months, he was in the actual Game, courtesy of financial backing he secured from a boyhood friend-turned-trader.*

*Unlike other speculative giants, Tony is not a fence-swinger. He handles size, but is very risk-adverse. His mathematical methodology was formulated by hand in pre-computer-model days, and then verified by a hired programmer. His data source was the thousands of transactions he had written on trading cards over the years.*

*His program's success has always hinged on a slightly-better-than-break-even performance over a vast latticework of open, interrelating trades. The approach is objective and conveyable. Within six years, Tony had shared his knowledge (plus trading capital) with a base of roughly 25 to 30 employees.*

*His company, Saliba Partners has a floor operation that trades as a DPM, (Designated Primary Market). The business, in other words, comprises "market makers;" traders responsible for assuming the other side of all incoming orders. Roughly 20 markets are covered, including Extreme Networks, Windstar Communication, and Walgreen's. The floor branch, headed by Tony's brother, John, holds memberships on the CBOT and Merc exchanges in addition to the CBOE.*

*The company also has an upstairs operation called Screen Based Trading, L.L.C., which is in partnership with a number of options order flow providers. Over the years, the business has developed widely used trading software.*

*At one time, Tony had planned to become involved on a grand scale with the training and financing of entry-level traders. Although the idea failed to materialize much past the initial two years, he hasn't entirely backed away from imparting his wisdom. He regularly writes for the "Trading-Markets.com" website and accepts periodic speaking engagements.*

*His major early loss, chronicled in* **Market Wizards,** *was colorful enough that I gave him the option of expanding upon it for this project, or discussing another incident. Tony replied via email that he had other stories—"you can't make an omelet without breaking some eggs." He decided to reveal his episode of greatest personal impact: one that had not been publicly recounted before.*

---

Tony Saliba still gets calls and email from trading-wannabes who read his profile in Jack Schwager's *Market Wizards*. The interview tracked him from an early confidence-shaking loss at the beginning of his career through his gigantic account runup in the Crash of 1987 and beyond. In it, he promoted an opportunity for young inexperienced traders to become part of his successful trader base, complete with financial and educational assistance. "I wanted to offer them the same chance I'd been given," Tony explained.

Unfortunately, as he put it, "That's ancient history. I've already been ripped off."

The deal-breaker was a loss Tony regards as his "most devastating." Unlike the usual war stories, this trade-gone-bad was being managed by employees. Tony has had some self-recrimination over how much latitude he was giving his people at the time, but other than that, he views the problem as having been pretty much beyond his control.

He wasn't even in the country as it was happening.

"I was traveling to Europe a lot on other business. I had put together a deal with a European bank which was interested in our software."

Tony's chief of staff, a man he identifies as "Ted," was charged with watching the accounts.

"He had specific and distinct responsibilities," said Tony. "And he had a clearly defined way to determine what the large positions (those of mine left over from the active trading days of the Crash) should do. He understood his job—at least he did while I was there with him.

"He would report directly to me. We didn't have email then, but he would call or fax to let me know what was happening."

Tony was carrying a large spread position in the S&P futures and options, and some additional options in the S&P 100s in his trading account. While he was away, Ted entered closing orders to try to trim the position.

For days, something in the accounts appeared to be "leaking losses." From his faraway vantage point, Tony couldn't gauge exactly what was going on. He knew the position they had on in SPX options was very large and intricate—thousands of spreads pointing in both directions. It included many "butterflies"—three-level option plays in which the middle strike (or "guts") is positioned opposite the high and low extremes (or "wings"). Relatively speaking, the overall trade didn't figure to be high-risk, although mere mark-to-market** swings could easily take a few hundred thousand out of the account one night and put it back the next without any trading being done whatsoever. Tony surmised that these P&L (profit and loss) convulsions were just something occurring at the bad end of a price swing. The account figured to come back into line.

"As the days passed, the leaking continued to get larger," said Tony. "At one point, the swing became tremendous; a quarter of a million dollars in two days, back-to-back."

Tony also had a young employee working the bond options. His trading was directed to be small and low risk.

During phone check-ins from abroad, Ted would maintain that the source of the interim bleeding was the SPX position, and that it should come back. Tony would hang up satisfied that nothing was going on beyond normal mark-to-market price ebb and flow. On the day after the second $250,000 ebb, however, the crisis became unmistakable.

"Usually, when something big like that happens, it comes back the next day," Tony observed. "This time, it not only didn't come back, it got worse."

---

**The value of a position based on that night's settlement prices

Tony was suddenly out a half a million dollars. Ted was swearing up and down, that the programs and reports were pinpointing the S&Ps as the source of the problem. Tony was not receiving a breakdown of what each individual account was doing. He hadn't set up such a safeguard because he hadn't anticipated a reason not to trust his lieutenants.

As the situation worsened, Tony's phone conversations with Ted grew heated. "I was screaming at him, 'how could you let this happen?' He was giving me a bunch of mealy-mouth stuff like 'I didn't realize, I didn't know...'"

Tony finally hopped a plane home from Paris. In sifting though wreckage upon his return and closing out all accounts, two facts emerged. One, he was out 1.2 million dollars. Two, the culprit behind the debacle was one of his young bond traders, a guy who had grossly overstepped his authority.

The trader named "Tim" had suddenly found himself in a bigger loss than he should have been taking. In a panic, he began chasing his position. For whatever reason, Ted was failing to monitor him.

"Tim was swinging from the hips two or three days in a row, just taking huge positions in the bond options, and some of the bond futures. His goal was to try to make it back in one fell swoop, but the hole he had dug kept getting bigger.

"He kept trading successively more contracts, five hundred in the morning, a thousand by early afternoon, two thousand after that. He was pyramiding (adding to losses) in reverses."

Suspicious that the same group of traders seemed to be involved in so many of the transactions, Tony instituted an investigation, eventually leading to the filing of charges. Ultimately, nothing fraudulent could be proven. Tony did win a monetary settlement that was to be paid back by the trader, but the chances were slim of anything coming out of it other than moral satisfaction. Today, Tony is left with unanswered questions about motives in addition to his many other recurring thoughts regarding the debacle.

"The loss was pretty difficult to take considering I didn't get the ride myself—it wasn't my loss...but then, it was. I didn't get a chance to trade off of it. It was a case of somebody else throwing a shoe in my shop.

"I've taken my own small losses along the way, of course. You get upset with yourself, you learn from it. You remember the feeling and you say 'I'm not going to do that again, I'm not going to step out of bounds.' But I've never had a spectacular blowup from my own trading.

"This time, with the other traders involved, what I felt was anger. It was a feeling of betrayal and disgust. It was like 'how could you do this to someone who was trying to help you?'

It was an ugly situation that nearly became violent. Upon his return to the states, Tony's first meeting with the rogue trader took place at his house.

"Tim pulled up in front of my garage. I grabbed a baseball bat, and was a hair's-breadth away from bloodying his skull. I swear, I've never been so enraged in my life!"

Tim started crying, which may have been what saved his cranium. In Tony's mind, it also gave credibility to Tim's claim that he'd done nothing deliberately nefarious. "I'd hate to think somebody could have faked tears like that," Tony observed.

He considers his ordeal to be a "defining moment." As a consequence, he shelved his idea of recruiting new trading armies. He also gained new insight into human nature.

"What people tell you, what they think, how they process their thoughts in terms of trading is all crucial to the business."

He added, with a hint of incredulousness, "This young trader actually thought there was a good chance he could make this kind of money back. He saw it leave his account in a day, so he thought it could just as easily come back."

Ted was similarly over his head, according to Tony. "He had just been given more authority than he could handle. He saw the situation as 'this is somebody else's responsibility, not mine—I don't want to be bothered with it.' When you have responsibility, you need to be prepared to have the buck stop with you." (According to Tony, Ted later made it clear that he was more interested in trading than monitoring someone else).

Tony imposed new safeguards on his command hierarchy, including intraday size limits. Computers make such tracking far more pragmatic today. They also made it possible for him to better define worst-case scenario risk.

"Options are inherently a more difficult risk to monitor because you can't size them up at a glance," said Tony. "Unless you have the proper tools and proper system, you can't monitor what the risk is at a given time."

Tony, of course, does have the necessary instruments, including software developed by his own company. "You can have direct control while being only indirectly involved."

Another adjustment was the implementation of an ongoing trader screening process.

"I have them actually write down in a diary or a log what they're doing, what they have on their minds. What is the beginning, middle and end of their strategies. Where would they expect to be in a best case, middle ground, or worst-case scenario.

You can see from their writings what a trader's mental framework is."

Tony confessed to giving much thought to the incident—rerunning it in his mind to a near obsessive degree. His whole trading approach is to mitigate risk, something 180 degrees at odds with the ordeal. His resulting anguish, not surprisingly, hit home in a profound way.

Still, he seems philosophical, almost charitable towards his onetime antagonists. Even at the time, his actions toward them might seem, to some, surprisingly tolerant.

"Believe it or not, I didn't even fire the trader. I suspended him while we were investigating him because I still wanted to give him the chance to explain himself.

"Ted stayed on with me for nearly a year after that, although the problem had become a major source of contention between us. It was hard to trust or believe him after that."

Still, Tony even gave him a chance to pursue his dream of trading in the pits. After six months, it was obviously not going to work out, but it's still interesting that Tony could offer such support after such a nightmare.

"We were all pretty young," he said. "I was thirty three, these guys were in their early-to-mid twenties. They were probably still growing and maybe even learned from their mistakes."

According to Tony, Ted is successfully managing in the trading business today. "People grow up," he mused. "Maybe he learned from what happened, maybe he painfully put it behind him, (or not so painfully, at least not as painfully as I had)."

As for Tony, his recent days have been blessedly devoid of similar excitement.

"We look to limit our losses. When they happen now, they aren't very interesting, but I'm happy not to be making the front page.

"I lost control then, and it hasn't happened to me since."

~

*Teresa Lo*

# Chapter 5

## Teresa Lo

### "I PRAYED FOR ONE THING—THAT WHEN I LIQUIDATED EVERYTHING, I WOULDN'T OWE THE FIRM ANY MONEY."

*That Teresa Lo isn't easily defined makes her profile both interesting and challenging, (the latter being that readily-pigeonholed people make less work for us writers). She's not a trader in a conventional sense. She operates off a screen in her house, but technical analysis only partially embodies her success.*

*She generally trades for only an hour and a half into the day—she's finished by 8 a.m. her time. (She's not even a typical all-American investor—she lives in the vicinity of Vancouver, British Columbia, Canada). She's in demand as a teacher-lecturer, but is more inclined to give live tutorials over the Internet than to appear at industry expos.*

*Probably Teresa's most defining market feature is her incorporation of the scientific method into her analysis. The approach isn't surprising considering her background; before getting her eventual BA in economics and psychology from the University of British Columbia, she majored in biochemistry.*

*"I thought I was going to be a dentist," she explained.*

*Today, she constructs scientific "if-then" hypotheses and applies them to the investment world. A given event will lead to a few possible outcomes, and Teresa makes it her business to ascertain the odds of any likely result. For her, technical signals are used to identify the "if-then" scenarios, not to serve as forecasting indicators.*

*"I use price and volume, and some psychology in my trading," she said. "I'm not in the prediction game—if we know where we are right now, that's good enough to make money."*

*She reflected upon the typical mix one finds wherever traders congregate—"the perma-bulls, the perma-bears who can only see the half-full, half-empty glass one way, never the other. You have people who are using technical tools incorrectly, or their mentality is colored by their dogmatic thinking."*

*It becomes hard for advisors to reroute their recommendations, especially when their opinions become more publicized, and therefore more necessary to defend. Their technical instruments become little more than excuses for their point of view.*

*Teresa's career as a solo trader began in 1998. Prior to that, she worked in brokerage houses for 12 years, most recently at Canaccord Capital Corp., Canada's largest independent firm. She was directly under the company's second highest official, Channing Buckland, Senior Vice President/Director, along with 14 or so other employees. They traded "everything that moved," according to Teresa, including stocks, futures, and currencies.*

*Teresa absorbed more than the markets.*

*"I had the advantage of working in a firm where I'd watch traders, brokers and clients blow their brains out. I began to recognize the personality characteristics that make people good traders."*

*At age 60, Channing decided to strike out on his own, but the then-33-year-old Teresa decided she was "too old" for such everyday corporate upheaval. She moved her operation into the quiet solitude of her home.*

*From there, she gained notoriety on the Internet. She loves its egalitarian nature.*

*"It truly is a place where, if you have an opinion, you can just give it," she enthused. "If you're around for awhile, and your opinions prove to be correct, it works out from there."*

*She frequently posted observations on the popular "Silicon Investor." Her own website, intelligentspeculator.com, has reputedly attracted a cult following. She was the featured cover story in "Online Investor," May 1999, and has been published in "Active Trader" magazine, as well as in the "Active Trader" section of "Fidelity Investment."*

---

There is a wide spectrum as to how a trader's Mega Loss impacted his or her subsequent career. Some of the stories present nothing more than an unfortunate market event; not related, in retrospect, to poor trader methodology or any later adjustment in technique. Others mark a sharp demarcation line, where the trader's actions can be defined and pinpointed as before/after the event.

Teresa Lo used to trade differently than she does today, but this isn't your typical event-leads-to-epiphany story. Not unless you count the second time she succumbed to the same adversity in the same way as her true point of transformation.

Teresa's loss stories take place in the late eighties, early in her trading career. Precious metals were experiencing some sharp upward blips in their otherwise relentless bear markets.

She and her fellow brokerage house employees routinely traded gold stocks—mining being a prominent industry in the region. They would compare charts of the major gold stocks with that of the underlying metal. Price moves would generally start in the stock sector.

"We'd see a little perk up in Newmont or Echo Bay," said Teresa. "We'd watch it for a couple of days, waiting to see if the bullion would confirm what the stocks were doing."

The signals would be small and perhaps not unambiguous, but other than anticipating the next spike, Teresa had no market plan. "I was a totally gut trader," she admitted.

As the stocks continued to surge slightly and then set back, Teresa steadily added more longs to her position. Her rudderless methodology made her vulnerable to the opinions around her. Gold seems to attract more than its share of bullish traders, partly because of its stellar historic highs, partly because it stays in the doldrums for so long, and also because it's—*gold,* with all the attendant splendor. Your spouse would much rather have it delivered on your front lawn than, say, pork bellies.

"Someone was saying 'we've got to press'," Teresa recalled. "We kept pyramiding."

The rally started getting significant enough to where it was being mentioned on the news. Technical analysts were bandying about wild projections.

"And then that would be it for the move," said Teresa. Unfortunately, she was already heavily invested.

"I knew the old saw about averaging up," she said. "I'd already learned to not average down," (add to growing losses).

Her additions were being implemented chaotically, without discipline. Teresa agrees with the widespread belief that the only sensible way to pyramid is for the initial commitment to be the largest, and subsequent increases to be successively smaller. When you're trading on emotion, however, the most hoopla occurs as the price becomes overextended—as your leverage is at its worst. Teresa's average entry level was precariously close to the high. Any kind of turnaround was going to cause pressure she couldn't have withstood. Her actual downfall occurred on a Monday reversal, (a day which closed lower after having taken out the previous high).

"I was wiped out," she said. "I didn't think it was a big deal. I was young and I didn't know much from trading. I thought, 'well hey, this is what happens, you either get lucky, or you don't' I just viewed trading as a big gamble, which is what most of the public thinks."

She also didn't understand technical analysis at the time.

"I thought it was voodoo. I didn't understand the fundamental nature of trading. How could you use the past to predict the future? But it was hard to understand those things because most of the people who trade are net donators to the market anyway. Even within the firm, there were all these misplaced conceptions about what trading and analysis were all about. I learned all the wrong things from the people around me."

Still locked in an inert trading mindset, Teresa moved to Canaccord Capital Corporation where she made friends with influential people. None, however, were particularly good trading models.

"Most of them were corporate financiers and salesmen. They didn't make a living from trading. They made a living from corporate finance fees and commissions. They were the croupiers in the casinos—the guy that flips the chips doesn't know much about gambling theory."

What they lacked in market savvy, however, they made up for in terms of other fast track access, and sometimes they brought their friends along for the ride. Teresa was able to assemble crumbs off their table into a $100,000 personal account. Who needed trading excellence under such circumstances? For awhile, understandably, her ambitions didn't extend beyond life as a corporate financier.

When gold fever struck a second time, Teresa again pyramided in the same ill-advised manner with the same unhappy outcome. The difference, of course, was that she now had $100,000 to blow.

When she heard a CNBC guest give wildly bullish gold projections one Friday afternoon, deja vu finally gave her an unsettling feeling. As the workweek was drawing to a close, Teresa remembers telling friends that the end was imminent. Unfortunately, it was already too late.

"I told someone that on Monday, we've got to off everything," said Teresa. "The guy said we can't, Monday's a market holiday. Of course, gold trades in London. On Monday morning, it gapped up on the opening and made one of those stunning reversals, but I couldn't off anything. The stocks weren't open.

"On Tuesday morning, we all knew it was going to be bad. I prayed for one thing— that when I liquidated everything, I wouldn't owe the firm any money."

Technically, her prayer was answered. When the smoke cleared on what once was a $100,000 account, ten dollars did remain. Teresa, who had had visions of being $50,000 in debit, was actually relieved.

"I had no more money. It all went on the trade. I wasn't good about money management at the time either."

But at least the event would lead to Teresa's long-overdue metamorphoses.

"I said to myself, 'OK, you're now 25, and you've blown out twice.' I decided right then and there that this was never going to happen again. And that I'm going to be in the markets forever, and so I'd better start figuring out what I'm doing.

"I decided that obviously, no one here knew what they were doing, or I wasn't very smart, or it was a combination of bad information and me."

She decided to go back to the beginning—wipe clean whatever conceptions she had had about the market. Her boss, Channing Buckland, introduced her to Ian F. Notley, an award-winning expert in cycles and wave theory. Notley steered her to a class that applied volume to technical analysis, and from there, Teresa's incentive kicked into high gear.

"I acquired a couple hundred books on stock trading, from the 1800s to the latest. I read every word of every book, and I distilled my own thing out of it. I used the scientific method to get a workable model of market mechanics."

She thinks that success hinges on being able to see the world as it is, not as you'd like it to be. You also have to be mature enough to accept what it's giving you. As a self-described "realistic trader," Teresa is concerned with probable outcomes. It's not that she has a high percentage of winning trades, but rather, "a high degree of getting it right in the construction of scenarios."

She determined that trading success is elusive because it is dissimilar to any other kind of success.

"Outside of the markets, you're trained to be tenacious, and to do things 'right.' If you change your mind, you're considered flaky. In trading, it hclps to revise your estimate."

Her rather esoteric ideas do dovetail nicely with the simplest, tried-and-true market axioms.

"Use a lot of money management. Don't be dogmatic. Takc your losscs quickly."

She amplified the loss subject a little further. Taking a big loss is a good way to be unable to recover, to blow out even. Losing everything on a series of small losses, on the other hand, is also theoretically not impossible.

"But if that happens," Teresa observed, "it probably tells you that your analysis method was incorrect."

~

*Laurence Rosenberg*

# Chapter 6

## Larry Rosenberg

## "I WAS BEGINNING TO BELIEVE MY OWN BULL----."

*In September, 1967, having just closed out a large, very profitable corn spread, Chicago Board of trade member Larry Rosenberg found himself position-less and carefree for the first time in months. He decided to take a stroll to the Chicago Mercantile Exchange where he'd owned a dormant seat for two years. It seemed like a good time to finally check out his investment.*

*He was like the husband who went out for a paper and never came back. Larry became a 27-year Merc floor legend. At one time or another, he has been prominent in every pit, especially the then-wild pork belly and live cattle markets. His usual style involved building up a large spread position, and then trading around it.*

*Larry quickly made friends, and became active in exchange politics. He was on the committee that inaugurated the International Monetary Market, the Merc's highly successful financial division. Seats were initially offered to the public for $10,000. Members were charged a mere $100.*

*He was elected Merc chairman in 1977, a post he held until 1980. "In those days, you served for the institution, not for the money," he said. "I used to warn against offering high salaries for the job. It just encourages people to focus on the money."*

*He helped develop the S&Ps, a market in which he and I have both have an active history. I had just suffered a personal slippage record—I was forced to pay 37 full points higher than my stipulated buy stop price as the Fed made another kamikaze, out-of-nowhere half point rate cut. Larry wasn't surprised by the mega-rip. Despite having once held triple-digit S&P positions, he considers today's volatile equities market a poor risk.*

*He permanently left the floor in 1994 to become a screen trader. The transition did not result in immediate success.*

*"I realized that a lot of the pit sense is auditory. Once you're upstairs, that's meaningless."*

*Another impediment was the kind of thing you hear all the time—his personal life was impacting his trading. He was going through a divorce. Typical of Larry, however, he worked through it and within three years, reclaimed his pit levels of return. Apparently, conquering another frontier was enough to satisfy him, however, because shortly after, he quit trading entirely. "No, I don't miss it," he declared.*

*Of course, it's not like he retired. Last July, he opened a business called "Intermarket Solutions" with his partner, Ryman Flippen, onetime vice-chairman and manager of Lind-Waldock Retail Discount Futures. The two basically offer their 67 years of combined expertise to act as a financial services consultant to brokerage houses. They aid their clients through all setup and operational aspects of their businesses.*

*"Between the two of us, I don't think there's a phase of our business that isn't 'been there, done that.' We establish relationships for people—we have tremendous contacts extending from here to Gibraltar. We can set up their businesses any way they want, anywhere in the world including offshore."*

*Larry can seemingly plug into any commercial situation with ease. He talked about how he recently ran a dot-com company. "It wound up where most of them do," he admitted, although he didn't seem concerned about the outcome. He was more interested in relating it to the current dire situation in which the Chicago exchanges find themselves.*

*"People talk about how in 2005, there will be 4000 exchanges," he said. "I don't know if there will be 4000, 2000, or 1000, but I'll tell you this. A year after, there will be four exchanges."*

*It's a situation directly relatable to Internet companies, or automobile manufacturers at the dawn of the 20th Century. "What were there at one time," wondered Larry, "two hundred automobile manufacturers? Three hundred railroads? Everything's that way."*

*The exchanges, particularly the Board of Trade, have recently seen their financial situations dramatically deteriorate. Seat prices have plummeted in recent months. Larry feels that it's going to take a major mindset readjustment for them to turn their fortunes around.*

*"The perception that if you want to trade futures, you go to Chicago isn't true any more. Geographic location doesn't mean a thing. It's as easy to make a trade in Frankfurt as it is here."*

*Aside from advocating that the exchanges apply a traditional business approach to their situation, ("Structure it like a for-profit company—hire a real professional to run things—let him make the hard choices, let him restructure, revamp"), Larry thinks salvation for the institutions will come from a new emphasis on what remains unique about them.*

*"Ninety percent of these so-called Internet exchanges are bulletin boards," Larry said. "I make a trade, and I don't know who's on the other end. It could be a serial murderer. But if I*

*trade through the Board or the Merc, I know I've got their clearing houses behind me."*

*In other words, emphasize security. That's what Larry thinks will keep the Chicago institutions among the final four remaining companies in 2006.*

*After a brief phone exchange, Larry suggested I meet him at his office. Being very people-oriented, he prefers face-to-face interaction; something cultivated during his years of supplying PR to press conferences. It was a good decision—the conversation in his scenic, 17th floor corner office flowed even more easily than his articulate phone interview.*

---

Larry Rosenberg is yet another self-described seat-of-the-pants trader.

"The times I probably got in the most trouble was when I overstayed positions because I'd become a believer. I felt I knew too much. It's really the markets that tell you what's going on. They're the sum of all information, so the market action tells you how to react. I reacted."

No one helped him develop his skills. "It was innate," he said. "I don't mean for this analogy to sound egocentric, but some people can sit down and play piano without being able to read music. I could take golf lessons for fifty years and practice every day, and I could assure you I still could never play golf like Tiger Woods.

"There's a certain sense—a timing. A lot of it is reading people, which is why I found the hardest transition to be from the floor to upstairs.

"I was successful very early on. I think my first year of scalping I roughly broke even. I basically made money ever since.

A lot of that I attribute to the fact that I'm a very disciplined person." (He doesn't, for example, deviate from his strict jogging regimen).

Consequently, he has rarely, if ever, found himself too far out on the high wire, but there have been significant losses. Larry built a successful career managing high level risk. Such a scenario isn't possible without a potential equally overwhelming flip side.

"I remember one time at the Board of Trade," said Larry. "I had a bean spread on. I was in the back months, and I was doing great on the settlements."

(Certain traders are entrusted with determining official settlements. When talking very sizeable positions, the bit of leeway they have within closing ranges could drastically affect their next day's account statements. Sometimes they're charged with determining the close of so-called nominal months—inactive contracts that maybe didn't even trade during the day, but would theoretically move to reflect the net changes of the active months. This often has major significance in spread positions).

"Then it came up near expiration on the front end of the spread. I was on one side, and Cargill, Continental Grain...whoever, was on the other.

"The nearby contract was expiring, going into the cash market. I was long that month and short a back month. The big players on the other side were short a delivery." (It was their intention to deliver beans against the expiring contract).

"There was a big cash interest, so obviously, the spread collapsed. I lost a lot of money.

"I told my wife, 'pack up David,'—at the time, my oldest son wasn't in school yet— and we went down and got a suite at the Fountainebleau Hotel in Florida. I had fun with the family. I never called the markets."

Indulging himself after losses was a recurrent practice for Larry.

"A lot of the presents I bought, I'd buy on bad days. That was a kind of therapy. Sometimes I'd buy a car, or expensive jewelry for my wife—something extravagant.

"I think it gave me a whole new outlook...an attitude toward losing. Namely, it's a part of life. It's not a terrible thing. I saw Michael Jordan play a lot of games, but I never saw one where he made 100 percent of his shots.

"It's easy to be a big shot when you're making money. But if you reward yourself only when you're in a hot streak, when you lose, I think you react much worse."

Packing up and leaving town was a favorite diversion. Rest, relaxation...and refocus.

"When I came back, I'd just try to put a winner on the card, I didn't care how small. I didn't care if I'd lost $20,000...$50,000. I'd come back and try to make $50. Get a plus day. That would get me back into a positive attitude." **

---

** My own experience makes me a believer in the psychological power of the strategy. A therapist treating me during my first potentially profitable year following a string of losers advised that I not allow the year to go negative. In November, as I started skidding back toward the even mark, he urged me to shut down until January. According to him, the subconscious would register any profit as a win—the amount wouldn't matter. The idea was, get a badly needed "W" into my yearly trading column...and my brain. Positive reinforcement would result. He was right. My streak was broken, and some of my best years immediately followed.

Larry learned early on to stop taking losses personally, ("You've got to get your ego out the way") although, interestingly, the adversity that bothered him the most was when investors in his managed funds would lose. After a sizeable run-up in wheat, he opened an account for friends and family members and his fortunes immediately reversed.

"I couldn't stand telling people they'd lost their money," said Larry. "It affected my own trading. I'd sit there and worry more about my uncle's two contracts than my own 200 contract spread."

Rather than face the unpleasantness, he assumed their losses in his own account. "From then on, if they wanted to know my opinion, I'd give it to them, but beyond that, I'd say 'don't tell me what you're doing. I don't want to know about it'."

His own losses obviously couldn't be as easily dismissed. He'd emotionally move beyond them, but at the same time, he'd view them as an educational experience. ("You don't learn anything from profits," he observed). Was there anything about the ill-fated delivery squeeze that Larry took away with him?

"I realized that I was beginning to believe my own bull----. I was BS-ing myself because I was settling the spread every night my way and collecting. That only takes you so far, and I think you could really say that was an epiphany.

"No one's bigger than the markets."

~

*Charlie Wright*

# CHAPTER 7

## CHARLIE WRIGHT

### "NO MATTER WHAT HAPPENED, I WAS GOING TO FOLLOW THE SYSTEM."

*Charlie Wright is the author of* ***Trading As A Business****, perhaps the last word on mechanical system trading. The content was derived from seminars he has taught under the same heading on behalf of Omega Research, creators of TradeStation. Charlie assisted in the early conceptualization of the program, and personally invented two key components, the Show Me study and the Tick chart. He has actively traded futures since 1982 and stocks since 1974. In the 1980s, he day traded S&P futures as a member of the Chicago Mercantile Exchange.*

---

To appreciate the full implication of a given trader's mishap, it often helps to understand what makes him or her normally successful. The irony of Charlie Wright's stumble wasn't that he's suffered significant losses; we all do. It's that his losses were destabilizing.. These days, Charlie tends to be positively robotic in the way he handles them.

For years, Charlie has been exploring evermore efficient ways to make losses an acceptable part of his overall program. He is perhaps the ultimate mechanical trader; one whose every decision is determined by a mandated set of rules that are not open to interpretation or fudging.

This approach gives him several fortifying tools. He always has a historical road map against which he can measure current activity. Either the loss or series of losses he is experiencing falls within the range of acceptable parameters, (based on what has been observed historically), or they don't. (They almost inevitably will, according to Charlie, unless something was done wrong in the testing). He doesn't have to make improvised decisions in the heat of battle. And he doesn't have to regard losses as something undesirable or at odds with a successful methodology. Losses are inevitable, and a mechanical system will consider them in all their fearsome glory.

Charlie acknowledges three mechanical trading approaches; trend following, support and resistance, and volatility expansion. Trend systems, (those that keep you perpetually in, and pay off when the market runs), are the easiest for most people to develop, including Charlie. Trading them, however takes resolve. Even a highly effective trend system will make almost all of its net profits in a mere two or three days out of any given average month. Another day or two will produce harrowing losses. Most of the remaining sessions will consist of relatively insignificant pluses and minuses.

"In other words," Charlie summarized, "most of the time, you're in a drawdown." The challenge becomes sticking with the program as it's giving you infrequent affirmation.

"In a mechanical trend system," said Charlie, "what you're exploiting is the notion of market facilitation. This goes back to Peter Steidlmayer's** core philosophical premise, which I believed was brilliant and changed my trading life. Markets have to facilitate trade to survive. To facilitate trade means they have to move, and I correlated that to the fact that they have to, at some point, trend and make a lot of money for the traders. Otherwise, traders wouldn't trade those markets and the markets would die.

---

** A renowned trader-advisor, perhaps best known for his development of the Market Profile.

"So you make the assumption that the prime directive of a market is to stay alive. Once you can be comfortable with that notion, you can then move to the next concept of how to be in for the big move, and how to survive during the sideways choppy market.

"That becomes a business decision, not an emotional trading one. You get to the question of how you're going to chip away at the cost of waiting, of being in during sideways, non-trending markets, and that becomes a business decision, no different than the decision of lowering costs of manufacturing."

In other words, losses are a mere cost of doing business, and in fact, Charlie regards them as more of a start-up fee than initial margin outlay. At least with account equity, you can use a portion to earn interest.

Not surprisingly, Charlie wasn't born with an innate complete system methodology. He recounts two reckless experiences early in his career; one that turned out good, but inevitably led to overconfidence and his eventual spanking.

In 1981, Charlie became adept at identifying market bottoms while under the tutelage of cycle expert Walter Bressert. His first trade was a comedy of errors, creating an unlikely windfall out of several trading blunders.

"What I didn't realize at the time was he [Bressert] had a whole bunch of stuff that you were supposed to do after you got to the cycle bottom." (MISTAKE ONE: acting on incomplete information).

Charlie identified an apparent cycle low in cotton, and purchased six contracts. "It went down about a half a cent, so I bought six more. Then it went down another cent, so I bought 12 more." (MISTAKE TWO: the classically ill-advised technique of adding to mounting losses, or "cannonballing").

"The markets closed, and my broker called up and said, 'I don't understand why you're loading up on the cotton market ahead of the report.' And I said, 'what's a report?' (MISTAKE THREE: to say the least).

"The next day, the report came out very positive for cotton, and it was limit up. I made probably $40,000 on that trade.

"So I thought, 'well, this is really easy, you just use Bressert's charts and find cycle bottoms and you load up and wait for the report to come out and make a lot of money.' (For another example of MISTAKE FOUR: see fund investors who have believed their inevitable destiny is to retire on eternally skyrocketing Nasdaq stocks).

"The next bottom I saw was in the grains," Charlie continued. "I started buying soybeans and corn...they would go down a couple cents, so I'd buy some more. I ended up probably with 20 corn contracts and 20 soybean contracts and I kept losing.

"Pretty soon, the $40,000 I had made in cotton was gone. The markets were still heading lower, and I started to get 'loser's anxiety.' I was losing my shirt. I finally realized that I did not know what I was doing."

In the middle of this five-alarm trade, Charlie decided to hop a plane to New York where his mentor was giving a seminar. After de-boarding, he learned, to his chagrin that corn and soybeans were both locked limit down.

A limit down price is the lowest an exchange will allow a market to trade in a given day. It's set in relation to the previous close; at the time, corn was allowed to trade no more than ten cents below unchanged, soybeans could not exceed thirty. In a lock limit down situation, sellers push it as low as the exchange will allow, and in theory, would be willing to sell lower. Unfortunately, the potential buyers recognize that the artificial price is too high, so no one steps up to accommodate the trapped longs. What's even worse is the knowledge that the market might be locked for several days, as has happened in the past. Each new limit down price is subtracted from the new close, i.e. ten or thirty cents lower than yesterday, and hapless longs see their accounts erode accordingly day by day.

"I told my broker, 'you've just got to get out of these as soon as possible'," said Charlie. Luckily for him, the first day's limit did not remain locked. He got out, losing roughly $20,000-$30,000 on top of the $40,000 windfall he also gave back.

He went to Walter Bressert's seminar, where he finally caught on to what he had been missing; namely, the technique of "setup and entry." (Something happens which sets up a potential condition for a buy or sell. The entry fill then occurs as the market moves in a second prescribed manner). This concept henceforth became a cornerstone of Charlie's trading approach.

If the grain experience were an example of excessive risk through overtrading, Charlie's next ordeal demonstrated the opposite. While it may never seem imprudent to throw in the towel on a given bad run, there actually is risk—even potential losses—in not sticking with correct trades. Charlie's most pivotal moment of all, by his own reckoning, occurred in the S&Ps after he had become a mechanical trader.

"I was trading ten lots. I did my normal day, and by noon or one o'clock, I'd had six losing trades. I was down $10,000-15,000, and that was a pretty heavy day for me back in 1984.

"I was very low... very depressed. I was literally ready to throw the computer out the window. I'd had enough, and I said 'how much money are they going to take from me? This is a terrible day! It's a choppy day, and I'm going to have to keep trading for another hour or two, and at this rate, I'm going to be down $20,000. I might as well save that extra eight or ten grand and give it up.'

"As I went through that thought process, something in me said, 'no, you're trading a system. If you give up, you're really not having the discipline to trade your system and you'll never know what would have happened'."

It's almost like traders have to snap themselves out of trances. Charlie went outside and took a five-minute walk.

"I made the resolve that no matter what happened, I was going to follow the system. I came back in and took another losing trade."

Still he was adamant: no improvising midstream. He decided that he would allow himself to re-evaluate his system and / or take a market break if both the current day and the next were losers. On this day, however, come hell or high water, he would stay disciplined.

The decision saved him.

"The market went through a huge rally. I made all the money back that I had lost and $10,000-15,000 more in the last hour of trading. And that was a *huge* influence on my life."

The experience affirmed what Charlie already knew about his approach. It was trend following in nature, so most of the trades involved would be flat to losers. This would be especially true in choppy, non-trending markets.

But, as the prime directive stipulates, the wins would come, and you'd have to be alive to receive them. You never know where the runaway moves will start—systems don't predict, they react. For Charlie to have not taken his prescribed large windfall would have been disastrous because the day wound up being one of those mere crucial two to three large monthly winners. To have missed it would have been to stray hopelessly from the path research had laid out. To have allowed the day to have evolved into a huge loser on top of it...

"That was the day I realized the value of system trading."

From then one, he hasn't looked back. His emotional concerns stretch no further than whether or not given losses exceed historical expectations. They almost inevitably do not, so he doesn't mess with the money machine.

In a field in which most everybody finds themselves learning hard lessons over and over again, Charlie is an exception. How was he able to transform himself almost immediately into a scientific trader without suffering the usual occasional relapses?

Charlie credits his business background with catalyzing his dogged pragmatism. His days pursing an MBA from Harvard Business School created an indelible influence. “They do wonders with your mind and how you approach business problems.” His trading is also reinforced by the fact that he owns a group of foundries; the Fall River Group. They manufacture brass castings, a process he sees as directly analogous to successful trading.

“I’ve always viewed trading as setting up the machine and spewing out trades like I’d set up the manufacturing machine and spew out parts. What I would never do is hire a bunch of people and say, ‘we’re making this widget. Depending on how you feel today, you can make it a different color, you can make it a different design, and we’ll go ahead and sell it.’

“It just doesn’t work that way. I wouldn’t do that in manufacturing, and I wouldn’t do it in trading.”

Charlie Wright stays disciplined in his trading approach because nothing else makes sense to him. Trading is not a game or a rush or a proving ground; it’s a process that generates income. All one needs are the necessary funds, the historical road map, and the mental leap that nothing else is necessary.

“You look at the markets as a statistical business,” he said. “I know that the market will move, I know that I will make the money, and I need to work on my system so that I’ll limit my losses during the non-trending time. I’ll maximize my profits during the trending times, and overall, I’ll have the ability to wait.

“In other words,” said Charlie, “I can take the drawdown. I’ve learned to love losses, and drawdowns are the investment required to get the return on trading”

Merton Feldstein

## Chapter 8

# Merton Feldstein

## "It's Not Hot Enough. It Can Never Be Hot Enough."

*Merton Feldstein is a forty-year veteran of the major Chicago exchange floors. He may well have traded in every major pit, and even some less-than-stellar ones. One of his more notable exploits was running up a fortune in the CBOT's short-lived ice broiler pit, (frozen chickens); a feat he accomplished in a mere two months.*

*He tends to make his home wherever there's trading opportunity. He reaped rewards in the exploding grain markets of the 1970s. When the embargo cooled them down in 1980, he thought nothing of relocating to the Merc and taking advantage of the cattle, Euro, and T-bill markets. He returned to the Board after Black Monday rendered the financial markets all but dormant, just in time for the drought of 1988. Today, he trades primarily corn and soybeans.*

*Such market hopping may seem like a logical enough strategy for any trader, but in fact, locals sometimes spend years staking out their pit positions, cultivating relationships with brokers, etc. One pit becomes home. They would rather weather declining volume than to have to relocate and start over.*

*Merton's not afraid of new frontiers. "I've always been sort of a risk-taker," he observed.*

*His trading style is a potpourri of pit savvy. He would be aware of what the large traders were doing, and sometimes he'd coattail them. He'd know the positions of the funds and the commercials. He'd use combinations of scalping, position trading, and spreading. He understood the various strategies; "pure spec scalpers" would want volatility, for example, "scalp-speckers" would look for unidirectional movement. He'd borrow a little from everyone—whatever worked.*

*"I've always had a bias though," he said. "Sometimes that was good, sometimes not." The direction wasn't; important just that there was one. "Just so I could see a light at the end of the tunnel."*

*Through the years, Merton has traded big enough to where the old exchange limits would get in his way. The floor has been good to him, though he doesn't realistically think pit life will go on forever. But as with his trading, he'll take whatever it has left to offer him.*

*"I just hope we stay dumb and hang on as long as possible."*

---

In George Orwell's 1984, "Room 101" was used as the ultimate weapon against political dissidents. Within it was the metaphorical and literal "worst thing in the world," a subjective horror varying from person to person. By the time the captors were threatening to unleash rats against the helpless protagonist, he wasn't about to resist anything—not even in the most secret recesses of his mind.

How do traders respond to losses? In as varying degrees as there are moods within each of us. Sometimes traders maintain their cool in situations that would utterly buckle most people and at other times, they sweat more than a casual observer might anticipate. (Then again, a casual observer is less likely to understand all the market ramifications that a seasoned pro digests).

Merton Feldstein recounted two occasions of extreme stress in his career. One cost him more money than he ever lost in a trading session. He regards that as little more than business-as-usual.

He didn't lose a dime in the incident that truly spooked him.

The realized-loss scenario occurred in the wild grain markets of 1988. A major drought hit in the spring, and kept the markets rocking and rolling throughout the summer.

"July beans had made a high of $10.99 and November hit $10.45," said Merton. "Then the market sold back to the $9.00 area.

"So, I got into a big position in corn and wheat, and a humongous one in beans. I had some bean bull spreads on—long July, short November, but for the most part, it was a Texas spread—long everything.

"That Friday, it was hot and the 6-10 day forecast called for much above-normal temperatures and no precipitation. I went home that night really happy. I'd had a good day, I had a good position on...I figured the market would be fantastic."

Commodity speculators don't apologize for the fact that adversity can bring them windfalls. Drought, war, whatever—traders didn't create the situations, they just react to them. Merton spent that weekend reveling in how bad the weather scenario (i.e. how good his financial situation) was likely to be.

"Saturday, it was so hot you couldn't believe it," he recalled. "My wife said, 'what are you so happy about?' and I said 'they're going to steam them on Monday. The markets will be limit up.'

"Sunday comes, and it's even hotter. I was on my sun deck, and I was just sitting there perspiring. My wife said, 'how can you sit out their, it's terrible.' I said, 'it's not hot enough. It can never be hot enough'."

Monday morning, Merton was shocked to hear that the pre-opening call was for lower grains. Why, he wondered, what happened? He was told that there had been overnight rains in the southern parts of the Corn Belt.

When a nearby grain contract gets within a certain time frame of expiration, the normal limit is removed entirely. July beans opened four limits lower—minus $1.20. The remaining active months in all the grains were locked limit down.

"You couldn't do anything," said Merton.

But how about the front month, which wasn't locked—did Merton bail immediately?

"No, I didn't jump ship right away. I didn't even get out the first day."

Merton correctly deduced that the markets were over-reacting as they often do in response to sudden news. By waiting a day before taking action, he managed to pare his losses, however slightly.

Still, it became his worst loss ever, and I figured we'd reached the heart of the Merton Feldstein chapter. Merton, however, didn't feel like there was much about it on which to elaborate. It was a loss, he didn't like it, but as he put it, "you can't win if you can't lose." Did it change him in any way; make him rethink his approach, his decisions—whatever? "Well," he deadpanned, "I guess it kept me from doing it again for about two weeks."

Merton might not even have been actively trading on the CBOT floor at all were it not for an event a year earlier. From 1980 up through October 1987, his floor of choice was the Chicago Mercantile Exchange. He was successfully putting on huge spreads in the cattle and Eurodollar markets, then, on October 19— Black Monday—he ventured into the S&P pit and traded up a storm. (Between five hundred and seven hundred lots, by his estimation. At the time, the contract was worth $500 per full point, twice what it is today).

During the session, he stayed focused on his trading. He was so intensely involved, he didn't know what his outcome was, but he was reasonably sure he'd done all right. He also believed that he had ended the session "flat" (without a position).

Hours later when he had the chance to reflect on more than the immediacy of his buying and selling, the awful significance of the day began gnawing at him. He'd just witnessed a debacle. That one session had busted out several locals and taken the bloom off the public's speculative mania. It would take years to recapture a similar broad-based participation. Trading houses were teetering. A fairly thriving contract, the CBOT's Major Market Index received its death sentence that day, although it would take years of a steady volume slide before it was officially buried. Talk of an ensuing depression was everywhere.

Merton's growing fear centered on a very specific market facet; the out-trade. Out-trades are transactions from the previous day that don't match up on the next morning's account statements. Two separate traders may think they sold when one actually intended to buy. They may not concur on which months or how many contracts were involved. Sometimes, they don't even agree on whether the trade transpired at all—you thought you traded with me, but I was signaling to the guy next to you.

Because of the nature of pit trading, out-trades are an everyday occurrence. Usually, only a clerical-like error is involved and both participants agree on how to fix it. Less often, there is a dispute over intent. The usual resolution in that case is, each trader assumes half of any resulting losses.

It's not a phenomenon that generally instills fear or dread, but this was a day in which the market spanned a ghastly 71 full points from high to low. (The average daily range in the eighties was less than five points). There were times during the day where traders weren't even sure what handle was being posted. (A handle in this specific case refers to 10 full point increments—for example, there might be confusion over whether the last price was 234.00 or 224.00).

"The S&P pit had a terrible, terrible reputation," recounted Merton. "You could come down some morning, and somebody would be claiming they made a trade with you that you didn't know about. People could have out-trades from days when they hadn't even gone into the pit.

"I started considering the consequences ... maybe they didn't know the 10 cards I thought I'd sold at 230.00. The December contract closed somewhere around 200..."

In that scenario, if that 10-lot sale was disputed, Merton would be facing, probably half of a $150,000 loss. With the amount he'd been trading, the situation could even be much worse.

"And I said, 'what did I do that for?' It was a stupid mistake, my even being in there."

The next morning, there were out-trades on his sheet—again, considering his volume, not surprising. Unfortunately, with the avalanche of problems everywhere, even correcting minor glitches was becoming a nightmare. Merton faced the 8:30 opening without a clue as to what his position was. He remained in the dark for a nerve-wracking half an hour.

He wasn't going to trade the S&Ps that day; he returned to his more comfortable Eurodollar pit instead. He did well, although he figures he missed major opportunities not being present for the opening.

"I just couldn't collect myself," he admitted. "Not while I wasn't sure where I stood in my S&P positions."

Two scenarios, strangely different, though both awful. The grain debacle set him back financially, but Black Monday unnerved him.

"I don't like to lose money, but if it's a regular situation, I just say, OK, I made a bad play. But to lose a lot of money that you weren't suppose to lose...

"I didn't really have a chance to worry about the beans. They just hit me over the head. Black Monday though..." He was quiet before giving his final summation.

"That was probably one of the worst evenings I've ever spent."

# Howard Malman

## CHAPTER 9

# HOWARD MALMAN

## "I'M TRYING TO BE SHORT A MARKET THAT BASICALLY HAS THE WHOLE WORLD CHEERING FOR IT."

*Howard Malman began his futures career in 1979 as a runner at the Chicago Board of Trade. Three years later he was trading in the corn and soybean pits with $5000 he had borrowed from his uncle.*

*Early on, Howard discovered something he would henceforth utilize in one form or another—the concept of relative strength-weakness. Spreaders thrive on it, but Howard was only trading one outright side. The measuring tool would tell him which markets to enter, and which to avoid. If he wanted to buy grains, he'd go with the strongest one, and vice-versa when he was bearish.*

*In 1983, the Board introduced its Major Market Index equities contract. Instead of merely comparing related CBOT contracts, Howard could now look at similar equity markets at other exchanges, as well as different market sectors, interest rates—a whole universe of financials. Within a year and a half, his relative strength approach had fortified him to the point where he could lease a Chicago Mercantile seat to trade in the burgeoning S&P pit. The spoos (S&Ps) have remained his primary market ever since, although today, he trades mainly off an upstairs screen. ("I'll still go to the floor when it's incredibly active," he said).*

*Currently he serves as Vice Chairman of the S&P pit, having been nominated by the Board of Governors in 1999. He also financially backs other traders, whom he trains and encourages to use his methodology.*

*Aside from trading, most of his time now is devoted to helping launch Carlin Futures, an electronic retail and proprietary futures firm. Howard is a partner with Carlin Financial Group (CFG), a direct access equity firm in existence since 1992. Under the joint venture, CFG is presently expanding into the futures business.*

---

In 1987, Howard Malman lived through an event that would forever shape the way he would trade. The stock market crashed, and he cleaned up.

"I was so enamored with being short," he said. "I made like ten times more than I'd ever made trading."

Leading up to the debacle, Howard was a fairly typical scalper. He always liked being short, but would be long also as the order flow dictated.

After the crash, however, two thoughts became embedded in him. One, it would be impossible to ever amass so much money so quickly by buying the market. Two, to be long was to always be vulnerable to comparable panic-induced sell offs.

"I never wanted to be long when something like that happened," said Howard. "I was always thinking that it could happen again."

So Howard developed a trading methodology that accomplished the all-but-impossible. In perhaps the greatest market ascension in all of history, Howard Malman prospered... by trading strictly from the short side.

It boggled my mind, I'll admit. I too have traded the S&Ps through the nineties and beyond. I've lived though the unremitting upside bias. There are several days I can recall when ten or twenty point intraday S&P breaks would be more than erased by the close. In addition to religiously following mechanical systems, I'd sometimes throw out an extra contract or two just to indulge myself. It was almost always a short, ("come on, enough is enough already!")—and almost inevitably a loser.

So how was it possible that Howard could flourish by seemingly fighting a relentless market every step of the way? For starters, no move is ever a straight beeline. Howard possesses an uncanny sense for identifying bear trends, however short and infrequent. He's not locked into the S&Ps. By noting divergence, he is able to take advantage of any given lagging market sector, such as the Dow or the Nasdaq.

He lets the premium futures-to-cash indicator of the previous close further determine his decisions. He also watches market fundamentals.

Also, just because he never buys the market doesn't mean he isn't adept at hitting the sidelines. "Learning when to step aside was probably the most important thing for me," he said.

Once he catches a downdraft, he mines it for all it's worth. Several moves have produced tallies of between half a million and a million dollars—sometimes within a single trading session.

His methodology has succeeded over a wide array of trading landscapes.

"From 1988 until 1993, the market went sideways," he recalled. "Selling rallies was fine—I made money.

"When the bull market started in 1994 to 1995, it became really hard to make money being short. There were very few days when the market traded lower. It was tough for me.

"Then in 1996 to 1997, there were some extended pull-backs that lasted anywhere from two to six weeks. I was able to take advantage of those situations. In 1998 to 2000, the market was obviously really volatile, and there were lots of opportunities to sell rallies and hit the top of the market.

"I've learned when to have one chip on the table, and when to have all my chips on the table. During this last period, (1998-2000) I was very comfortable with managing the size of the wager I was willing to make. It started coming easier."

There was, however, one significant bump in the road during that time frame. Alan Greenspan. If there ever was a person on earth who could create a market "melt-up"—a mirror image of a crash, it's our current Federal Reserve chairman.

"In October, 1998, during the Russian crisis, and the long-term capital crisis, I was so bearish that I thought the world was ending. I was short everything, and things were going pretty well."

The market had been trading lower all week, and Howard was profiting. The weekend approached, during which he was slated to appear in his brother-in-law's wedding party. He left the floor early to have his tuxedo fitted.

"I was at the tailor, in the basement getting the legs shortened. There was about a thirty-minute period where I wasn't even calling to check. I was standing there while the guy was chalking my tuxedo.

"At 2:30, I called the floor to see where the market was. They gave me a price and I'm like, 'what are you talking about?' I thought the guy was reading me the wrong month. They told me the Fed had cut the rate. This was maybe the first time I'd been exposed to a rate cut during the middle of the day.

"I was short about 50 full-sized S&Ps and I lost $600,000 in five minutes."

He was unable to watch the market. In any event, he generally doesn't believe in hesitating when wrong.

"I've never been afraid to take a loss. But I'm also not afraid to get back in at some point, even if I'm getting back in at a worse level. It's never too late to get back in."

Howard swallowed hard—and bought back nearly his entire position at the highs. "I kept five on, just to spite myself," he said.

He was then forced to endure a weekend of social obligations while his mind was a million miles away.

"It was horrible," he said. "I had to stand up in my brother-in-law's wedding and the whole weekend, it (the loss) was all I was thinking about. I kept telling my wife, it was the most expensive f*****g tuxedo I'd ever bought!"

His brother-in-law didn't take the sentiment personally. He'd worked for Howard for a time and therefore understood market dynamics.

Howard's wife, Tracy, has also been supportive—a crucial trading advantage, as has been recounted frequently. Her loyalty, however, has been tempered with some emotional self-preservation.

"She told me a long time ago not to tell me what was going on until we were broke or retired," said Howard. "She said she didn't want to take the ride in-between.

"My parents both passed away between three and five years ago. Besides my wife and in-laws, they were the only two people in America that rooted for the market to go down every day because they knew I was short. My mom was always so happy when she turned on CNBC and the Dow was down 350 points."

His small coterie of boosters aside, Howard's eternal market position has proven rather lonely.

"You have to understand, I'm trying to be short a market that basically has the whole world cheering for it. You're fighting everybody. You're fighting every mutual fund owner that has money in the market. You're fighting the president who wants to get re-elected. You're fighting Alan Greenspan who wants to keep his job, you're fighting Bob Rueben. Money rules the stock market. There are always going to be underlying reasons for it to go up."

He laughed. "Nobody...*nobody* wants this market to go down. It's not like crude oil or metals or currencies where there are people and opinions on both sides. If you want to fight a market like this, you've got to be like a gladiator. You've really got to have a chip on you shoulder." He laughed again. "Which I do."

It should be noted, however, that despite the fact Howard's professional trading is 100 percent from the short side, in his overall life, he is not so lopsided. Like so many other Americans, he has an equities portfolio.

"The trader part of me is cynical and pessimistic," he observed. "When I saw the market go up and up like it did in '97, '98, '99, the trader part of me knew it wouldn't last.

"As for the investor side of me... was I putting money in the market? Was I investing my kids' college funds? Absolutely. It was too hard to resist.

"But knowing that I was in the pit to be short and make a lot of money meant that I wasn't as scared having money in the market. If I owned a bakery and had a lot of money in the market, I wouldn't be able to sleep.

"I was able to, at any moment, hedge my position in one second. It was like I was trading my own personal hedge fund. But I would always...*always* be rooting for the downside."

Howard Malman will never be caught the wrong way in a crash. His personal 1998 waterloo, however, has been merely the first of three or four times as of this writing that the Fed has cut rates unannounced. The upside is now vulnerable to runaway action in a way Howard perhaps never foresaw.

"From that day, I've learned not to mess with the Fed," he said. "Whenever there's even rumors in the market about the Fed coming in, I tread lightly. I rarely go into the FOMC meetings with a big position, because I know they're capable of any type of surprise."

Aside from that, he remains comfortable with his unusual relationship to the market.

"It's too hard to be good at everything in this game," he said. "I think you've got to try to be good at one thing. You're either a guy who likes to be long, or you like to buy dips, or you like to buy rallies....

"I can't pick bottoms, I can't buy rallies. My attribute is, I know when the market feels like it's toppy, and I know when my formula adds up to making a big wager.

"I try to be a specialist." He smiled. "Too bad I didn't specialize in buying dips. I'd have five times more money than I have now!"

*Adrienne Laris Toghraie*

# Chapter 10

## Adrienne Laris Toghraie

## "Give Me All the Obsessive-Compulsive People You Can."

*Considering the pervasiveness of market losses and the people who suffer them, it isn't surprising that there now exists a thriving trader-specific branch in psychology and behavior modification. Many traders willingly plunk down often substantial amounts of money to discover what it is that internally blocks their paths to wealth and success. They reason that anything that can get rid of their demons will offset the admission fee many times over in trading profits. Some maintain that indeed, their investment gamble paid off, sometimes to life-altering degrees.*

*For fifteen years, Adrienne Laris Toghraie has been coaching business professionals on how to improve their careers through Neuro-Linguistic-Programming (NLP). For the last twelve, she has accepted clients exclusively from the investment community, and recently, has made her screening process even more stringent.*

*"I now only take people who have a system or methodology they believed would work if they could follow it," declared Adrienne. "They have to have shown some major discipline in their life. They have to have a burning desire for wanting to make changes, and they have to show a desire for wanting to work with me."*

*In one way, her acceptance process has gotten more liberal. She no longer believes that all-encompassing mechanical trading systems are the only path to success; in fact, she contends that the top level traders are discretionary. At the time of this writing, she was about to teach an advanced seminar on intuition in Sedona.*

*"In order to have intuition be reliable," she qualified, "you have to have a foundation of mechanical technical information."*

*Through NLP instruction, Adrienne applies uniform behavior modification techniques to each trader's specific methodology. The resulting hybrid provides the client with a custom-made blueprint for success.*

*Neuro-Linguistics refers to neurology, (the nervous system) and language. The program seeks to alter negative behavior resulting from embedded, subconscious beliefs that are incompatible with successful trading. Adrienne, one of the more celebrated NLP coaches, has a client list spanning the globe. She has lectured at numerous business seminars, and has appeared on CNBC.*

*Her services include two private open-ended day sessions, which go from morning until midnight if need be. Her current fee is $6,500.*

*She has written seven books including* ***Get A Life: Treasure Diary For Creating Wealth and Happiness and The Winning Edge: How to Use Your Personal Psychological Power in Trading and Investing****, which she co-authored with Jake Bernstein.*

*Adrienne has no personal losing anecdotes, although she has obviously been privy to numerous accounts from others. Her inclusion in this book is because the dynamics of losing are complex and elusive, a phenomenon few people understand or articulate better than Adrienne.*

---

"I work with changing people's perceptions at a subconscious level," said Adrienne Toghraie. "Usually, when people change things at a conscious level, it's not going to be so powerful that it will change their lives."

This is why she won't specifically chronicle her methodology in books or interviews. It isn't just the information itself that is important, but also how it's presented and received.

"If I were to say to you, my whole seminar is "create your own reality,' that is the bottom line. But in order to get the experience out of it, so it is meaningful to you enough to apply towards higher levels of success, you need to go through a certain process."

Traders come to Adrienne in order to change their condition. Their primary complaint is trading losses. The root of their problem, however, inevitably extends into other areas of their lives. The fact is, "loss" as a specific trading situation is analogous to more general negative experiences.

"If you think of anything in your life that you perceived to be negative, it had to do with a loss," Adrienne asserted. "A chronic loss situation has to do with chronic low energy. When you break the body down to its most elemental components, what you have is space and vibration. The high level of vibration is the vitality that keeps you at a peak performance level."

Success depends upon balance in a person's life. That doesn't necessarily mean that equal time has to be spent on each facet, but rather that each area must support the others.

"If you are physically, mentally or emotionally depleted—everything within you is working synergistically to support the low state. I call it the cesspool."

It probably is no great revelation to most traders that a bad outlook, for example, is going to negatively impact their performance. I nearly drowned in my own personal cesspool, which I chronicled in my first book, *Market Rap: The Odyssey of A Still-Struggling Commodity Trader.*

Years ago, I had received a trading-related compulsive gambling diagnosis. I was told that my only hope was to abandon the profession I had fought so long and hard to enter; a decree that challenged some of my deepest self-perceptions.

Yet despite my resolve to not take the warning lightly and to not act like a typical person in denial, there was a part of me that felt it was just too simplistic. Yes, I seemed to be out of control a lot, and yes, a lot of the screening questions seemed to relate directly to me. Yet, how do non-traders really get into the trading mindset? How do they jump into our unique world? My market behavior was being correlated to people going crazy at racetracks and casinos. To me it didn't seem analogous—or fair. I knew there was more to my market life than "addiction"—I had enjoyed success in system development, which, unlike the therapists, I refused to discount.

For whatever reasons, I was able to resist and re-group, and my financial situation has significantly improved since then.

I don't say this with arrogance; I know it's never inconceivable that the other shoe could drop. But my confidence is pretty freestanding these days, although I must confess to a twinge of satisfaction over getting validation from Adrienne.

"What I discovered about the best traders in the world is that they're all obsessive-compulsive," she declared. "In fact, that applies not just to traders, but to any highly successful person. It's easy by other standards of therapy to say the person is a gambler."

In Adrienne's book *Trader's Secrets*, co-authored with Murray Ruggiero, an investor is tracked through a series of seminars. According to Adrienne, the result was that he turned $2000 into $10,000 after the first one, and then after seeing a second guru, he ran his money up to $150,000 before suffering a $75,000 drawdown. Adrienne's point was that a traditional diagnosis during the 50 percent retracement time frame would likely be that he had obsessive-compulsive, or gambling instincts.

The problem, according to Adrienne, is how the verdict overlooks the fact that the man's gambling mentality—even his high degree of risk-taking, was an integral component necessary for such high returns. Rather than eliminate obsessive-compulsiveness, Adrienne advocates re-channeling it. In doing so, she purportedly helped take the man from his $75,000 level to over three million dollars.

"We made him obsessive-compulsive about being risk-adverse, about following his method.... about taking care of himself in such a way that would support his trading."

"Yes, give me all the obsessive compulsive people you can. These are the people who are going to be successful."

Success involves re-alignment in many areas, including health and nutrition. While not flat-out denigrating psychiatric mood drugs, ("I'm sure there are many good psychologists and psychiatrists who are doing a lot of good for a lot of people,") she leans more toward natural herbs and meditation. All in conjunction with Adrienne's therapeutic methodology.

When someone is going through major trauma; divorce, bereavement, etc. Adrienne suggests scaling down position size. To those who would argue the financial impossibility of such a move, Adrienne countered, "You can't afford not to.

"Pulling back on your trading, cutting back on your risk—that becomes a balance too. You have to nurture yourself; you have to pay more attention to your health and emotional stability.

"Too many times, I've seen traders who say they have to maintain their living wind up in a worse financial position then they would have been if they'd taken care of themselves."

Miserable people are the most likely to sabotage themselves. It's as if the person's very being gets fatalistic about the very idea of success—"Why are we fighting for this? What's the point?"

It may be that intent and corresponding action are more at odds in the trading world than anywhere else. Adrienne works with people who can't take a signal, who take too many, or who can't follow their systems even when historical performance charts should be fortifying them. Those outside the business may find it bewildering, but those within need no elaboration.

"Whatever level you're at, whether we're talking relationships, health, money, your career, there's something between you and that next level. Sometimes it's a conscious choice where you say, 'I'm happy where I'm at right now.'

"It's when you're not happy that you can discover that what's between you and that next level is you."

*Pat Arbor*

# Chapter 11

## Pat Arbor

### "IT'S BETTER FOR THE BOARD OF TRADE TO SURVIVE ELECTRONICALLY THAN TO FALL ON THE SWORD OF OPEN OUTCRY."

*This one was intimidating.*

*Pat Arbor is a Chicago icon, much like Oprah'n'Michael J'n'Sammy S'n'Kup. To write his introductory paragraphs would be to wade through a mountain of credentials, and then throw out those which would serve as a lead paragraph in most anyone else's profile.*

*Currently, he operates his long-held clearing corporation, Shatkin, Arbor, Karlov and Company, which includes the Octagon Electronic Trading Group branch. He actively trades as he has done for most of his life. His office is not without the ubiquitous price monitor. He has served on the board of directors of more than one bank. He is an author and lecturer, a man who has, on a regular basis, huddled with Mayor Daley and Chicago's political elite. Actually, he was a mayor himself— of suburban Harwood Heights, Illinois. Before that, he taught high school math and economics.*

*His greatest fame was his stint as the Chicago Board of Trade Chairman, 1993-1999.*

*"They were the Golden Years, if I may say so with some immodesty," said Pat. "We had record volume in five of my six years. Our seat prices in May of 97 reached $857,500, an all-time record." (Full seats have recently traded near the $300,000 level). "I may have had nothing to do with that, it may have been a confluence of events, but like Clinton, I have to claim credit for it."*

*He was turning out to be every bit as colorful as people had been advising me he would be. I'd never received so many tips on how to present myself.*

*"Don't show up like your usual rumpled Columbo self," said one friend who had had a few Pat Arbor encounters. "He's a dapper guy—appearance counts with him." (I promptly removed my somewhat irreverent black and white checkered tie and put it in my pocket).*

*Others hoped I would broach subjects not particularly relevant to this book. Pat Arbor's social life, for example, has received some attention over the years. To put it gingerly, he was never alleged to have been shy. (He's an exuberant newlywed today). I didn't pursue any of that, although I had to smile over his observation that trading was "a very seductive business—like a woman. It just kind of wraps its arms around you and seduces you."*

*But, he added perhaps ironically, a good trader doesn't succumb to the lure. He doesn't "get married" to a position.*

*Pat's other big passion is mountain climbing. His office is lined with several colorful photos of him and fellow climbers standing atop various pinnacles including the Matterhorn, the Eiger, and Mt. Kilimanjaro.*

*I had a few moments to absorb the office decor (which also featured a large photo and a painting of the CBOT building) as Pat wrapped up some phone business. He was speaking in Italian during his last call, and the personal section of his resume confirmed that he is fluent in the language, as well as an "aficionado" of the culture.*

*"I describe myself as 'Unca, the last of the Mohicans,'" he said when I requested an assessment of his administration. "I'm the last person to have chaired the Board of Trade as the world's largest futures exchange. For 150 years, we reigned supreme, but because of one word—technology—we lost our number one status."*

*Pat doesn't feel that the slide was inevitable. In his mind, America could still be the primary hub of futures activity, if capturing overall business were a bigger priority than merely protecting the open outcry system.*

*Under his tenure, the Board linked with London's open outcry LIFFE exchange. It would unfortunately prove similar to teaming up with a nation in the process of becoming occupied.*

*"Eurex annihilated LIFFE," Pat said. "When I saw the Germans take the Bund (German bond) contract away from LIFFE with lightning-like speed, I said, 'because of technology, that could happen to anyone'."*

*That prompted him to forge an alliance with Eurex. It was a personally satisfying achievement, but ironically, one of the factors Pat believes cost him a fourth term. His opponent, David Brennan, initially campaigned against Eurex; music to the ears of open outcry proponents.*

*"Then he did a flip-flop about three or four months later and embraced Eurex," said Pat. "It cost about twenty million dollars to shut it down and re-boot it up again."*

*To the floor members clinging to their traditional way of doing business, Pat offered the following observation.*

*"I don't like electronic trading any more than I like losing my hair. There's not much I can do about either one. It's better for the Board of Trade to survive electronically than to fall on the sword of open outcry. That has been my mantra."*

*Pat Arbor has never been one to mince words, and he's not too charitable toward his immediate successor, (who has since been defeated by Nickolas Neubauer).*

*"Brennan was the wrong guy. We've now lost not only our number one mantle to Eurex, but the Merc's going to beat us this year because of the things he's done. We should be trading e-minis on the Dow contract. We had stuff like that on the burner."*

*Among his other criticisms was the large sum of money the Board paid to release President Thomas Donovan from his contract, and the twelve million it spent on restructuring "with nothing to show for it."*

*Pat asked me what the title was of my previous book. I told him* **Market Rap: The Odyssey of a Still Struggling Commodity Trader.** *In a non-offensive, almost breezy manner, he observed that other artist-writer types he's known over the years— a sculptor friend, for example— typically didn't enjoy trading* *success. There's something about artistic temperament that's at odds with the capitalistic mindset.*

*For years, I've suspected as much.*

---

"My trading career got off to a spectacularly bad start," said Pat Arbor. "I bought one soybean contract and stood there for two weeks and watched it go down $2,000. That was around 1964 or 65.

"For the next five years, I had some ups and downs...never really made any money, and by 68 or 69, I had lost it all. I had to actually leave then because I was broke, and in fact I owed money. Quite simply, I didn't know how to trade."

He was able to book one significant winner—the seat he was forced to sell for $17,000 had originally only cost him $10,000. As with so many others though, the markets weren't about to let go of Pat forever. He re-entered the game in 1970.

"This time, I had to pay $31,000 for the seat. It was probably the best trade I ever made," he laughed.

He had to borrow the $31,000. His intent now was to become a broker, which he regarded as less risky than trading.

He wound up flourishing in both capacities due to the incredible exploding volatility of the seventies grain markets. His eyes were opened wider this go-around—things were clicking in his head.

"I noticed that the fellas that drove the nice cars and had the nicer homes and wore the nicer clothes and seemed to be more successful were those who spread. At times, speculators would do very well, but it seemed they had these big cycles up and down. They'd go from one extreme to the other. The spreaders seemed to do consistently well."

One day as Pat was filling orders, beans dropped to lock limit sellers. On an individual contract basis, January was 34 1/2 cents lower than November. That's the difference you would have faced in theory if you would have bought and sold each contract individually. (In practice, you probably wouldn't be able to sell the limit down side).

Just as there are always bid-offers on each contract, however, there are also spread bid-offers—a single price differential relating to the two contracts. Obviously, the spread offers are usually close to or exactly at what the two contracts are yielding individually, but every once in a while, the two sides get out of line—sometimes way, *way* out of line, such as when a mistake is made.

That's the lucky accident Pat suddenly encountered. On the price boards, the limit down January contracts were 34 1/2 cents under the limit down Novembers. In the pit, the spread was being offered at a mere 17-cent difference.

"A big grain company came in and bought 500** November soybeans," said Pat. "I managed to sell them 100 at limit down. I went over and bought the January limit down."

---

** In 1998, the Board revised their system so that grain orders were bid and offered in actual contract sizes, just like every other commodity. "Three bid for 20" now meant you were looking to buy 20 contracts. Prior to that, grain bids and offers were always done in multiples of five—you couldn't bid anything less than a five lot, which meant one contract, 10 meant two, 100 meant 20, etc. It was weird shorthand for the fact that all standardized contracts were comprised of 5000 bushels. Therefore, you would offer to buy or sell "five," meaning 5000 bushels, or one contract. In the above example, the house "buying 500 " was actually buying 100 contracts. Pat's bid for 100 meant he was purchasing 20.

Mission accomplished on the outright side—Pat had bought January bean 34 1/2 cents under November. He then offset his position on the spread order in the pit; buying the November and selling the January for a mere 17-cent difference. His profit was gigantic, risk free and nearly instantaneous. Pat stared at his trading card as one might scrutinize a multimillion-dollar lottery ticket.

"I made $17,000 without even blinking my eye. I turned my card over and looked at it every which way, and every which way I looked at it, I had made $17,000!"

It was such a laugher hit that Pat suffered some pangs over whether he was actually entitled. He went over to the grain disk and informed the broker who bought the 500 Novembers what had transpired. The broker assured him that the trade was legitimate.

"He said, 'New York told me to buy November, and that's what I bought'."

It was a gigantic windfall for Pat at the time. The next day, while reading his inflated account statement he concluded, "If one of the world's biggest grain companies could make a mistake like that—not understand spreading—then I may be able to make money spreading!"

Almost immediately, Pat was able to build himself a respectable financial base. He paid off his $31,000 debt. Again, the markets were wild centers of opportunity, but he also had another advantage. Many of the veterans were complacent about the big gains they'd make in the morning hours. They'd leave for the day, and Pat would finish out the rest of the session as the pit's primary market maker.

He became particularly adroit in so-called "carry" or "old crop-new crop" spreads, which involve two different months in the same market. Under normal conditions, deferred months are priced higher than the nearbys. The disparity results from the "cost of carry;" the amount of money needed to accommodate storage costs, interest rates, etc. over the time difference between the two delivery dates.

Futures prices, of course, vacillate and so do the spread relationships. If the price of the deferred exactly equals the price of the nearby plus the carrying charges, the spread is said to be at "full carry." It will trade narrower than that, particularly if there's an immediate demand for the crop.

Rarely, however, will the spread exceed it much, because such a situation would create an incentive for farmers to not immediately deliver. They'd realize they could get higher prices in the future over and above their expenses, so they'd hold their product off the market. That would create a demand for the nearby months, which would then rally relative to the deferred, and the unusual price situation would self-correct.

It's therefore considered a safe play to buy the nearby and sell the deferred month as full carry is approached. The opposite side of the trade would be regarded as one of high, indefinable risk. This was the unfortunate position Pat took sometime in the early 1980s.

"I started selling the old crop-new crop spread. It kept going against me, and I kept selling more."

He was assuming the side of the potentially unlimited liability—selling July, buying November. Calendar-wise, the two months were in the same year, but in every other way, they represented two different harvest seasons.

When he initialed the trade, July was "considerably under" the November—presumably, knocking on the full-carry door. By the time he was done adding to the position and was forced to exit, the nearby had actually become more expensive than the deferred.

On the surface, it doesn't seem like Pat had had a sensible risk-to-reward situation to start with. Consistent with a recurring theme in this book, outside influences were keeping him from trading with his usual sharpness. When his son encountered teen-aged difficulties, Pat was beside himself with worry.

"I was so immobilized because of my personal family problem that I had to turn to my partner (Henry Shatkin) and he had to liquidate the position for me. I told him I couldn't pull the trigger; get me out!  It was a terrible time. It took about two or three days to untangle the mess. It was a difficult position to un-wind.

"I was affected psychologically. I had a lot of anger and a lot of self-destruction."

There was also a touch of macho, exacerbated by Pat's emotional state. There was one primary trader on the other side, who seemed intent on luring Pat deeper into the trade with in-creasingly tempting bids and offers. Pat's job was to pounce on that which seemed out of line. It got frustrating as seemingly good edges kept failing to pay off.

In looking back, Pat regards the trade as being a case of not recognizing changing conditions. The long November, short July side of the market had been working well for a while, but Pat had the misfortune of being mentally vulnerable when the corner finally turned.

"The trader on the other side was very in tune with the cash markets,' said Pat, "but he seemed to be giving money away down there. He was paying above the market for the spread.

"He had information that I didn't have, but I never traded on information. I just traded on gut, visceral instincts. But I think he kind of dressed it up for me a little bit."

Pat didn't consider his position to be career threatening at any time. "Just painful and costly." It put him down significantly on the year, which any trader can tell you is an unpleasant mindset to have to endure. The fact that Pat Arbor got past his times of trial is a matter of historical record.

"I learned to keep my inventory smaller," he said. "I learned furthermore that if I was having troubles outside the Board of Trade, I would not trade."

As he has done during other trying occasions, Pat took some time off following his memorable event. He stayed close to his son who straightened out and currently enjoys a successful brokering career at the Merc.

Today Pat runs his many business interests and trades off a screen. He still consistently thinks in terms of spreads, even if the "legs" are not as pure as they were in his pit days. He had the misfortune, for example, of being long the S&Ps during the week of March 12, 2001, the biggest weekly drop to date, but he managed to mitigate some of his losses with the sale of out of the money options.

"That's probably the biggest problem I'm having these days," he laughed, "that I'm long the S&Ps."

However the market resolves itself, Pat Arbor will no doubt not be thrown. For one thing, he understands something that he didn't in the early eighties.

"Sometimes, if you've got a problem, you do things that are goofy. You try to immerse yourself in the markets to blot everything out. People put themselves in bad situations in the market just to get their mind off other matters.

"The trading game is very psychological," he observed. "We don't know why we do things sometimes."

~

*Mark Cook*

## Chapter 12

# Mark Cook

### "It was like I was tied to a post, and they were shooting at me with shotguns."

*Mark Cook is one of the few market celebrities who can trace the bulk of his earnings to his personal trading account activity. He runs twice-daily recommendations for Cook Advisory, sharing what he considers to be high probability ideas in the bond and equities markets with subscribing individuals and institutions. He started doing so in 1993, in response to requests from his readers.*

*"I provided commentary for the Striking Price Options column of Barron's magazine from 1992 to 1996," said Mark. "People would call and ask if I had a service."*

*Nevertheless, Mark emphasized, "I trade my own money and that's it. I don't manage any other funds. Trading has been my primary source of income for the past 12 years."*

*Mark grew up on a farm, and later got involved in market investing; a common route considering the relationship between agriculture and futures trading. His interest from early on, however, was financial-related—first stocks, and then stock options. He began researching the latter in 1980. He developed an approach of selling premium and then buying it back after prices withered under usual time decay.*

*"The probability of making money selling and then buying was a lot higher than going in the other direction," he observed.*

*He sold both puts and calls with equal enthusiasm. Most option buyers eventually surrender their funds in much the same fashion a casino will drain a combined player bankroll. Just as the house seeks ever more customers and maximum hands dealt per hour, Mark was believing that he couldn't sell enough. He started reinvesting all his profits and continued writing ever more premium. The strategy consistently worked until the day the steamroller closed in on the dimes.*

*The most notable result of Mark's Cities Service debacle was that it turned his option strategy around 180 degrees. Among other resulting modifications—prior to 1982, he was a seller of options, hoping to capitalize on normal price deterioration over time. Since the incident, he always buys first and then sells only to liquidate longs. He won't even get short on a covered basis, (for example, simultaneously selling a nearby option and buying a further out strike, which makes the risk finite). By implementing a relatively narrow strategy, he can now quantify his risk to an exact degree; an impossibility when one assumes the opposite, unlimited side.*

*Since adjusting, he's enjoyed his largest and most consistent returns. (Starting in August, 1987, he has reputedly racked up a few million-dollar months). He keeps his profits separate from his original principal—the gravy is never used to finance bigger positions. Funds removed from the investing table, more likely than not, funnel into his many farm and land purchases. He rests easier when his gains become a hard asset. Also, he loves his picturesque, rolling Ohio landsite, probably more than trading.*

*Mark's notoriety grew in 1992, when he won the options division of the U.S. Investing Championship. He did so by launch-*

*ing a campaign Eisenhower would envy; his business plan outlined, itemized, and prioritized everything he knew about markets, history, and his own personality. He didn't, for example, make any moves on Friday—15 years of historical review convinced him that his net performance on that day was negative. For similar reasons, he halted all activity during the entire month of June.*

*Throughout most of the year, he ran neck-and neck-with a high-risk pyramiding trader. As with the Tortoise and the Hare, however, Mark maintained a consistent pace, believing his gunslinging rival would eventually self-destruct.*

*In November, Mark decided his performance-to-date was adequate, so he shut down while his rival made a failed bid to keep pace; unable to overcome Mark's 563 percent annual return.*

*Mark is profiled in the recently released Jack Schwager book,* ***Stock Market Wizards.***

---

"You're hitting on some touchy, sensitive areas," Mark Cook observed about the theme of this book. "Traders aren't self-deprecating as a rule. They like to see themselves as being invincible."

He was being philosophical, not contentious. His epiphany happened 19 years ago after all, and he's come a long way since.

His point was well taken. One pretty much needs a healthy ego to take on markets. Although speculators are natural pontificators, personal failure— however temporary— is hard to reconcile with their oft-projected Air of Trader Grandeur.

Despite a few closed doors, however, speculators overall made themselves accessible. They provided a wide array of losing scenarios, complete with prologues, epilogues, a window on their psyches, etc.

There are degrees to every aspect of the losing experience, as varying as humanity itself. More than anyone else I encountered, Mark's experience caused a total trading metamorphosis. The 1982 event formed a demarcation line in his career. He had one methodology before, and a distinct, in some ways contrary one after.

The shift from option selling to buying is the obvious case in point. Writing a detailed business plan and understanding his risk thoroughly at all times is another. He is always aware of his worst-case scenario, and if it strikes him as excessive, he won't commit.

Perhaps most significantly, he stopped pyramiding after 1982. ("It produces the maximum exposure at the worst possible time.") He now consistently removes his profits from his account. The money designated for implementing strategies is fixed from the start of the year.

"I want to be able to live to fight another day. Had I always done that, Cities Service wouldn't have been the debacle it turned out to be."

Consistent with what I'd heard frequently recounted, Mark had been flying at his highest level-to-date just before his plunge. In those days, he was trading on a skinny account— $20,000-$30,000. He made money every month in early 1982, which he would then pour back into his war chest to fund ever-larger positions. In May, trading his biggest size yet, Mark earned a heady $50,000, which he immediately converted into even larger personal exposure.

"As we entered into June," said Mark, "I was selling naked calls against Cities Service higher than where it was trading. I was anticipating that the stock would not appreciate by the expiration in June above where I'd sold the calls," (and therefore, they'd expire worthless). "I figured I had probability on my side.

"I was over-exposed monetarily. I was under-prepared as far as the ramifications of the severity of what could hit me."

Gulf oil announced its offer to buy Cities Service, and instantly, the highest strikes Mark had written were $20 in the money. (And as crushing as they had become, the mountain of shorts written at successively lower strikes were obviously even more devastating).

"They stopped trading the stock— the exchange halted it— and I couldn't buy the calls back at all. The people I'd sold to could exercise their options, which they did," (making Mark short). "By exercising, they were dumping a lot of their stock, which I had to buy " (at the now hyper-inflated prices).

He couldn't react at any rate—trade was halted. He had to meet margin that he didn't have. For a man who relied so much on shaping his own destiny, such helplessness was excruciating.

"It was like I was tied to a post, and they were shooting at me with shotguns."

There was no telling whether the resumed trading would result in even higher levels before he could act, but in a sense, the point was becoming moot. Mark had just lost a half million dollars that he didn't have. Minus the $165,000 his account had been worth at the onset, he was suddenly $335,000 in debt. He had also lost $100,000 respectively for accounts he was managing for his mother, father and aunt.

Luckily, he had supportive relatives; his parents lent him $200,000. Also fortunately for him, he had already owned farmland, which he used to secure a bank loan on the remaining debt.

"There's nothing more humbling than borrowing money, and putting it in an account, and having it automatically just get sucked," Mark said. "I'd put the money in to get my net worth back to zero. There was no chance of borrowing to recoup the loss; it was just used to cover what I'd already lost in order for me to be able to walk away."

At 28, Mark faced the prospect of working his way out of a large hole. There was no more trading equity. He worked his farm and brokered—two full-time jobs, and finally secured enough money to resume trading nearly two years later. He was on his readjusted program now, slowly re-building from a new $25,000 stake. By the late 80s, he was again able to support himself exclusively through his own account activity.

The solid family support behind him helped— it's a recurrent theme throughout this book that external environments impact trader performance. Mark's wife, Terri, sympathized with her husband's angst, but someone in the family had to maintain "business-as-usual." She set up a strict monthly budget.

For some reason, fellow traders weren't charitable at all. "They asked me how I could be so stupid; didn't I see this coming?"

A scan of news items was part of Mark's daily routine; it was a factor in how he computed volatility. He had therefore been aware of the rumors, but he maintained, as did Linda Raschke, that not even an actualized takeover should have produced such a dramatic response.

He couldn't find much in the way of professional commiseration until years later when Linda and Larry disclosed their own experiences. Finally Mark realized that even other pros had fallen victim. In 1982, however, not much was bolstering his outlook.

"I thought I was a bad trader, a failure. I thought I didn't know what I was doing, and I was clearly out of sorts."

His emotional evolution approximated what psychologists recognize as stages of grief.

"My first reaction was disbelief that it was happening," said Mark. "Nothing about the makeup of this particular trade, after all, had been intrinsically different than any other. Same indicators, same methodology. It just happened to be the one that got me, not unlike a lightening strike that kills the person in the middle of the field.

"So then I began experiencing rage—that I'd been victimized, (and I still believe that to this day). The third thing I went into was total submission—belief that I was a dunce. Fourth was the recovery or rejuvenation...of picking up the pieces. I decided I was not going to quit. I wanted my money back. I thought that I still had five years basic experience under my belt, and I would somchow bc ablc to twcak thc situation.

"That's when I really turned the corner as a trader."

~

*Linda Bradford Raschke*

# Chapter 13

## Linda Bradford Raschke

### "It's like comparing battle scars with each other, to prove that you have earned the right to be a gladiator in the marketplace."

*Linda Bradford Raschke is often associated with two things; the S&P futures market and day trading. Linda, however, isn't comfortable with any such pigeonholing. First of all, she almost always holds positions overnight, so she's not technically a day trader. Second, she is not married to the S&P market. She loves the contract's relatively large size, plus its volatility. ("Volatility equals opportunity. Opportunity equals profits.") She also feels that its myriad of inter-related components make it tape-reading accessible in a way not found in other markets. Still, she'll regularly have positions on in currencies, grains, energies, and metals—anywhere she perceives opportunity.*

*Like Mark Cook, Linda is a renowned figure (profiled in Jack Schwager's* ***The New Market Wizards****) who offers market services to clients, but derives the bulk of her income from personal trading. She started her career in 1981 as a market maker in equities options. She was on the floor of the Pacific Coast Stock Exchange at the time, which is also where she was trading* *during the Cities Service near takeover. She would later move to the Philadelphia Stock Exchange, and finally to trading futures onscreen from her personal office.*

*During the 90s, she had $35 million under money management. Three and a half years ago, she took a hiatus to, among other things, build a house and barn in Florida's Palm Beach area. (Training horses is one of her passions).*

*She is now resuming her managed funds. As for her own market activity—it's doubtful she'd ever be long removed from that.*

---

Probably the word that best describes Linda Bradford Raschke is "unflappable." She faced her most harrowing market experience at the tender age of 23, and she's as matter-of-fact recalling it as she presumably had been experiencing it.

"I was fairly tough and resilient in those days," she explained. "I had to put myself through college and worked from early on. I had a double major. My parents divorced when I was sixteen.

"I was a survivor. I'd already developed a fairly thick skin."

That skin would be tested, along with the mettle of several other traders, on June 17, 1982. Linda had been floor trading on the floor of the Pacific Coast Stock Exchange for less than a year. She was under the wing of another trader who had supplied her initial stake in exchange for the usual financial remunerations. That Linda came into the day short premium was not unusual for someone in her position.

"On the Pacific Coast Stock Exchange, probably ninety percent of the market makers were premium sellers, including my mentor. That's what I was taught how to do"

She also learned to search for options that appeared over-valued.

"At Cities Service, the implied volatility was extremely high. Of course, that was because it was rumored to be a takeover stock, but we were still playing it anyway. Then the news came out."

In those days, market volatility was a fraction of what it is today. The Dow was under 1000, and the modern bull market was still a few months away. In that environment, Linda wouldn't anticipate how such a violent response could occur even if the takeover did materialize. Unlike Lawrence McMillan, Linda couldn't think of any previous market event to which she could draw a parallel.

"I was still extremely young and new to the business. I'd made some money trading, but not enough to sustain this type of loss. It took me out of the game. My account went to a deficit."

Linda's was primarily short straddles in Cities Service, i.e., she was selling both calls and puts at identical strike prices. Such a strategy blows up when the underlying price movement is dramatic enough. In this case, Linda's unlimited exposure in the calls would be nowhere near offset by the money she'd collect from her decaying puts.

She was also positioned in several other Pacific Coast Exchange markets, which made for an awkward situation the next morning.

"I had to go down on the trading floor and walk into each pit and shut down all my positions. It was mildly humiliating."

The takeover cost her roughly $85,000. She was suddenly around $40,000 in debt to her clearing firm. She was young and new to the business. She faced a substantial personal debt, and her backer was out his seed money. It would have been understandable, to say the least, if she'd become a little unhinged.

"No," she countered, "it was more like, 'oh Linda, look at the mess you got yourself into now'."

She had enjoyed a brief period where she was just getting out from under student loans. Just before her trading days, she'd gotten hired as an $18,500 a year financial analyst. It was a good deal for the time. Now suddenly, she was under yet another financial mountain.

"It was depressing," Linda conceded. "I didn't have any professional skills—not like a doctor or a lawyer or an accountant. And when you come off a salaried job that pays you $18,500 a year, and you have no skills and you *owe* $40,000, let alone you have to make your living expenses..."

It was tough, but typically, not destabilizing. Linda acts like she can't even comprehend any course of action other than soldiering on, let alone actually succumbing to despair.

"I figured, OK, I'll just have to go back to living like a student for awhile. I negotiated a deal with my clearing firm to pay them back $1000 every month. They knew that I was a good trader who just got caught in an unfortunate situation. I lived frugally for the next year or two."

Almost immediately, a New York trader who wanted representation on the Pacific Coast Exchange worked out another financial arrangement with her. She was trading again as if she hadn't missed a beat. Within a couple of years, she was again operating off a respectable financial base.

She has since taken bigger hits, (notably, $100,000 on Black Monday), but the Cities Service event stands as her most destabilizing personal loss.

"It wasn't that I was using sloppy habits or knew I was doing things that I shouldn't do," she said in retrospect. "I just made a novice mistake of having too much leverage."

The experience did not sour her on the idea of being aggressive at the right times, however. In Linda's mind, money management is about more than risk control and keeping losses in check.

"It's also about when you have a choice situation, when all the chips are falling right into the palm of your hand, and you'd better step on that gas pedal. Because, after all, 85 percent of a professional trader's profits might come from five percent of his trades."

As her option career moved her from San Francisco to the Philadelphia Stock Exchange floor, Linda became more adept at lessening the exposure inherent in premium selling. She'd buy distant out-of-the-money calls and puts as protection. Also, like Mark Cook, she learned how to better make the long side of options work for her.

Today she trades futures, and handles risk through a close monitoring of leverage, correlation in her market portfolio, and support and resistance levels. She is far more conscious of following the prevailing trend.

Typically, Linda was able to take positive, instructional elements out of her harrowing experience. She had survived her worst-case experience. Subsequent small losses became easier to take due to how they compared to the Big Hit.

"You learn that the game is not about money; it is about learning your own limitations and overcoming them," said Linda. "It is learning about endurance, fortitude, and building character. It is about learning how *big* the marketplace is, and how small and humble we must be in its shadow."

Linda added that when such a situation arises, "love of the game" is what keeps one committed to persevering. Learning to claw your way back from adversity becomes incorporated into what makes up your very identity as a trader. Once you've been under such fire, it's as if you become part of an elite fraternity.

"It becomes difficult to relate to people who have not experienced the same degree of intensity or pain," Linda observed. "Most professionals I know talk about their losses and their bad trades but they never talk about their good trades. It's like comparing battle scars with each other, to prove that you have earned the right to be a gladiator in the marketplace."

She continues to step up to the plate whenever the opportunity is right, citing that as the one characteristic that separates good traders from exceptional ones. Of course, confidence, perseverance and maintaining an unemotional grounding don't hurt either.

"You know, you get out of bed each morning, put on you shoes, go to work. Hope that the sky is blue. Focus on the immediate task at hand. I'm going to trade today." Linda laughed at the simplicity of it all.

"You just have to keep moving forward."

Larry McMillan

## Chapter 14

# Lawrence G. McMillan

## "It Looked Like It Was Just Printing Money."

*Lawrence G. McMillan is an aggressive options trader, lecturer and author of considerable renown. His 1980 book, **Options As A Strategic Investment**, is widely considered to be the Bible of option trading strategies. (The third edition was printed in 1993). More recently, he wrote **McMillan on Options**, and currently edits and publishes two newsletters, "The Options Strategist" and "The Daily Strategist." Both identify derivative product opportunities in equity, index, and futures options markets. He also provides "Daily Volume Alerts," a fax/email update that uses equity option volume to pinpoint short term stock trades.*

*These services are all part of McMillan Analysis Corporation, of which Larry, (as he prefers to be called), is president. He founded it in 1991. For most of the prior 15 years, he was in managerial positions at Thomson McKinnon Securities, Inc., New York City. At the time of the Cities Service scenario, he was heading the Equity Arbitrage Department. I asked him for his definition of arbitrage.*

*"It's buying a security, and selling it, probably in an equivalent form for a better price. You could buy stock, and then sell the equivalent form of options at a higher price, locking in a little bit of money. That's classic arbitrage.*

*"Risk arbitrage is where, say, one company is taking over another for stock. You buy the shares of the company that is going to be taken over and sell short the (higher priced) shares of*

*the company that is going to be issuing their stock. If the deal goes through, then both sides of your arbitrage become the same stock, and you're out."*

*The latter was more or less Larry's strategy in June of 1982. His Cities Service story was beginning shortly after Linda and Mark began facing their respective nightmares. The slight difference in entry time resulted in three people losing big on opposite sides of the market.*

*Again, we're talking "risk" arbitrage.*

---

The difference between Larry McMillan's story and that of most of the rest of the people in this book is, Larry didn't face his ordeal alone. He was an institutional investor, albeit the department head, who was implementing a corporate policy. Whatever other anxiety he would experience, he didn't have the added burden of having to second-guess himself, at least not to the degree of a maverick trader suddenly losing his roadmap.

"We were arbitrage and looking for companies to be taken over," said Larry. "Once a company receives a takeover bid, it doesn't trade up to its full price immediately. There's a spread between the actual closing price of the deal, and where it's trading in the marketplace.

"Usually the public gets out at that point. If you were holding Cities Service at 30, and all of a sudden it's trading 55, you don't really care if it's going to be worth 60 or not. You just sell your stock and take your profit."

To the Thomson McKinnon Securities, Inc. Equity Arbitrage Department, the probable trade trajectory after 55 was the whole point. The brief time following a takeover is where there would be almost certain opportunity to lock in money.

"We started to accumulate some pretty big positions in the stock at that point, somewhere in the 54-55 neighborhood."

It wasn't a textbook arbitrage case of stocks being bought and sold on different sides of the takeover because the offer was going to be settled in cash. The players were simply speculating that what they were paying in the market would be lower than the ultimate buyout price. Larry noted with a chuckle that the reason there are now more of the classic stock-for-stock variety transactions is because today's suitors generally don't have the necessary cash.

As an additional strategy, the department also began selling deep out-of-the money puts. The instruments offered a scant payoff ranging from between one and four points. It was more than the arbs felt was deserved, however, which was the point of the sale. The options represented small but highly probable profit opportunity, and things could only go wrong (albeit significantly so) if the underlying stock dropped dramatically. (Dimes in front of the steamroller).

"Between the long stock and short puts, we had on the equivalent of 250,000 shares," noted Larry.

In those days, there was a lengthier allowable time frame between when a stock had to be tendered (turned over to the acquiring company) and the final disbursement. Two to three weeks transpired between the two dates, according to Larry's recollection.

It must have represented an eternity to the multitudes hanging their fortunes on so many variables. Cities Service was undergoing wide price swings in the cash market, which was irrelevant to anyone who'd already tendered their shares, (including Larry). They'd surrendered control to Gulf. Meanwhile, rumors began circulating that the deal was going to fall through.

On Friday, August 6, nearly seven weeks after Cities Service had begun trading at the inflated mid-fifties level, Gulf Oil confirmed that it was backing out. The tendered stocks all had to be returned to the investors, which allegedly took about a week. Trading was again halted.

On August 9 McMillan's group could actually trade Cities Services—they again possessed their stocks— but the opening price was a harrowing 30. In what will be seen many times throughout this book, the big hitters did not dump immediately. They instead assumed the risk of waiting—letting the hysteria die down—before searching for a more optimal level. They did, however, take immediate action on their options.

"We covered all the puts we were short and actually went long puts to protect what stock we had."

They couldn't buy all they needed for a hedge, though; they were bumping up against position limits short of that. They were, however, able to lessen their exposure by about 80 percent.

The re-opening day held as the low of the resumed trading activity. The department was still holding onto the stock when, a couple weeks later, Occidental Petroleum announced another attempted Cities Service buyout. The McMillan Arbitrageurs could now exit at 48.

"We ended up losing about two million dollars, which was a lot better than it had been at one time. The day it had opened at 30, we were long roughly a quarter million shares at 56."

That had represented an open loss of six and a half million dollars.

Larry doesn't, in retrospect, fault anything in the way of decision-making or execution. The takeover looked like a done-deal, and it was his job to take action accordingly. Several huge arbs, such as Ivan Boesky, were doing the same thing.

"There was no way you could have done any kind of research and found out that Gulf Oil was going to back out of the deal. Even if you could have, you probably would have already tendered your stock and wouldn't be able to get it back.

"It looked like it was just printing money. Our attitude was that we thought the deal was going through, and it looked like a lay-up." He laughed as he added, "Obviously, I'm a little more cynical now."

While the logistics of the trade may have seemed beyond reproach, Larry did become more conscious of leverage after the experience. "You can always do a better analysis of worst case scenario. In my own personal trading, I definitely set new limits on the amount of risk I would take on any one position."

He admitted that being part of an arbitrage situation did mitigate some of the standard Monday morning quarterbacking.

"We were a trading department. We tried to go back to 'business as usual' because risk arbitrage trading is a profitable business."

And, according to Larry, Thomson McKinnon as a whole stood behind its arbitrage department, which made the happy epilogue of one month later possible. In another takeover—this one involving Martin Marietta, Larry's team had initially bought the stock and, because they didn't think there would be a big price on a takeover if one in fact even occurred, sold calls against it.

The rumors started getting "a little stale," according to Larry. Martin dropped below the strike's 35-strike level. There was one week to go before expiration.

"Then we saw someone really aggressively buying the stock options," said Larry. "So we figured maybe the takeover was coming after all."

Larry's supervisor asked him for input. Larry replied that their easiest bull play would be to just cover the calls, and hold their stocks un-hedged. The superior replied fine, but don't just cover half—go for it all.

"We made back a million and a half—almost everything we lost on Cities Services," said Larry.

It's always darkest before the dawn. And vice versa.

*Jack Kotz*

## Chapter 15

# Jack Kotz

## "I JUST WALKED ON THE FLOOR AND HEARD THAT NOISE."

*"One of my kids mentioned that all through high school, she thought we were poor." Jack Kotz laughed at the memory. "I asked her, 'didn't you wonder about that when we were taking vacations and flying seven or eight kids with us?' 'Oh,' she said. 'Nah, I always thought we were poor'." He laughed some more.*

*The girl had maybe been keying on her father's self-effacement. Jack would try not to bring losses home, but if a day were really terrible, "I might have said something." At any rate, the idea of him bragging around the house or anywhere else seems unlikely—his daughter probably didn't hear much to counter the occasional grumbling.*

*Maybe her perception was borne out of her unpretentious upbringing. Nine children were raised in a warm, supportive environment, complete with vacations and unlimited educational opportunities. Some of the more ostentatious trappings of prosperity, however, were absent. There was no professional lawn service; the kids were responsible for that. They shoveled snow off the driveway and got jobs as soon as they came of age. To keep them down-to-earth, the parents made a conscious decision to avoid moving to such upscale Chicago suburbs as Wilmette or Kennilworth.*

*"They always worked," said Jack. "They all work today." (All four of his sons have market-related careers). "And no matter what happens, they'll make it. They'll pick up the pieces, and they'll go on."*

*He echoed the sentiment I'd encountered elsewhere—that traders initially handed large startup bankrolls tend to be poor candidates for ultimate success. "People who have known at least some economic hardship are less likely to be afraid of failure when it hits."*

*An admirable environment, certainly, but Jack defers domestic credit to his wife, Darlene. "She's been very good to me. She always let me do pretty much what I wanted to. She never complained when I lost money, or took advantage when I made it. We both give each other a lot of freedom. And she was just great with the kids."*

*Jack, in return, never questioned his role as breadwinner. The images of his wife and children would pop into his head whenever his trades threatened to get out of hand.*

*Jack epitomizes the old-line Board of Trade grain trader—one who was around when the floor was more of a small, close-knit community, a time when the veterans lent a hand to the novices, and smoking was allowed at the edge of the pits. The Merc's bellwether live cattle futures was a thriving CBOT contract at the time. Soybeans traded in eighth cent increments, and 20 cents generally represented a yearly move. A career could be launched for a mere thousand or two.*

*He arrived in 1958 while still in college on the Army GI Bill.*

*"I was on the train heading for the Midwest Stock Exchange, and I got off the at LaSalle Street station and walked into the Board of Trade. I said, what the hell, 'grain market,' let's see what this is all about."*

*No one in his family had known a thing about the futures business, including Jack, (although he had been trading stocks from a young age). He went upstairs to the Daniel Rice and Company office and asked for a job. He was told the company wasn't hiring, so Jack offered to work for free. He somehow knew instantly—this was the place to be.*

*"I just walked on the floor and heard that noise," he said. "It was like being in a giant crap game."*

*A year later, he graduated from college and bought a membership for $4,650. "Within a week, it was down to $2,600," Jack laughed.*

*He was then engaged to be married in a few months; already motivated by domestic realities. His initial stake was about $1000, which he nurtured as best he could in the soybean pit. He simultaneously hustled for other incomes; everything from in-house clerical work to outside-jobs selling insurance and mutual funds. He also brokered for several years.*

*Through it all, he got to know everybody. He was the most commonly suggested subject for this book by grain traders. "I know I have to talk to Jack," I'd reply. "I just feel funny about pushing him."*

*Some of his friends are everyday people like me. Others are wealthy, powerful industry celebrities. Jack requested I don't name-drop them—he's protective of their privacy.*

*Others routinely feed him detailed market information, although without being privy to the other side of his phone conversations, I've wondered what it is about them that could stretch out to a half hour, an hour or more. My guess is, for Jack, interpersonal exchanges rarely tend to be "all-business."*

*Today, he spends most of the year in his Florida home. (He returns to the floor during the spring and summer). Our phone interview was interrupted twice by calls from his children, and another three times from God-knows who. He screen trades futures and stocks on a daily basis. He plays tennis, dines with family and friends, and in general, enjoys life.*

---

Considering his background, Jack Kotz's Mega-Loss might seem a little out of character. It was a gigantic, immediate hit. Jack usually derived his profits from more consistent market grinding. He would not be shy about building up large positions, and yet there was normally that guiding, inner voice keeping him from getting too leveraged.

There were some mitigating circumstances behind his stumble, however. For one, he had just run up the quickest, biggest open profit of his life. In six weeks, during the same 1988 drought that would eventually catch up with Merton Feldstein, and untold others, Jack had amassed over two million dollars. There had never been a better time for him to put his pedal to the metal.

For another, no one could have anticipated that on that one horrible Monday, the nearby soybean contract would open four limits down. Jack would have weathered a limit or even two without too much problem. But four? It was ridiculous. What kind of rain scenario should have instantly taken so much out of such a highly stressed crop?

All kinds of weird shouldas-couldas-wouldas figure into climactic trading events. Jack might have held onto his windfall had it not been for, of all things, his good nature. The Friday before the Monday collapse, he was at a friend's house in Colorado. The friend was also heavily committed to the long side of the grain market, and was on the phone buying more as the close approached. Jack had actually been thinking of sidestepping the weekend by cashing everything in on the close, but felt it would be bad manners—kind of like betting on the "don't pass" line when your friend is holding the dice.

But what the hell, he thought, if he had to give up 20 cents on the opening Monday, no big deal. He'd still lock in a fortune and besides, the weather figured to work more in his favor over the weekend. He still believed in the market's underlying bullish potential.

As his friend piloted the two back to Chicago Sunday night, Jack didn't give much significance to the fact that rain was dogging their whole trip. He just felt he'd have to concede 20 or 30 cents. He hit the floor Monday morning and asked for an opening call. A dollar to a dollar and a half lower, he was told. To which Jack could only reply *"What!?"*

Jack was long all the grains. No short legs within bull spreads—nothing but straight-up longs across the board in beans, wheat, corn—at or near exchange limits. He was also long calls which, prior to Monday, had been looking to pay off significantly.

In one day, his entire two million dollar-plus profit was wiped out. True, he was no worse off than he had been six weeks earlier, but the suddenness and magnitude were devastating.

"Emotionally, it really affected me," said Jack. "It was like taking a sledgehammer and hitting me in the stomach."

Jack was haunted not only by the loss, but also by the fact that he'd toyed with the idea of cashing in. Besides that, the event had occurred at such an outrageous time. The Friday weather reports had called for perhaps the hottest weekend of the year with not a trace of rain expected anywhere.

And of course, watching a position vanish so quickly, one that he had so skillfully and methodically worked into such a profit, would be a shock to anybody. There would be a lot of nagging regrets in days to come, but Jack's immediate concern on the fateful July morning was taking action.

"Like anything else, I did what you do—picked up the pieces. I bit the bullet, got out and salvaged what I could."

He didn't take time off afterwards; that wasn't his style. Prior to his semi-retirement, Jack would be the last one to miss a trading session. (One day, he hopped a train after a winter storm stranded his car. He was one of only a handful of members who made it in, and the exchange closed shortly thereafter).

Still, his trading approach was suddenly different—it would almost have to be. The giant Bull Run opportunity was terminated in one day. He was back to grinding it out on a much smaller scale.

"I was pretty gun-shy for a while, I can tell you that. It took me a long time to re-group"

It would be a tough hand for anyone to be dealt, but Jack weathered it stoically. When he acknowledged that in our business, "money is a way of keeping score," there seemed to be a trace of irony.

"I know guys worth millions who aren't happy...in fact, they're miserable. I know other guys who haven't got a dime, and you'd think they just won the U.S. Open or something. You play your own game—you don't worry about hitting 370 like Ted Williams, you hit your own 250, and you'll get where you want to go."

"You have to be satisfied with yourself," he said.

How would he describe his current status, I wondered—retired? Nope, protested Jack, he's trading every day, just smaller than he once had. Don't refer to him as retired.

"When I'm dead a couple of days, then I'll be retired."

*John Baca*

## Chapter 16

# John Baca

## "I'M GRABBING HIM, AND THERE'S SPIT FLYING EVERYWHERE."

*In my first book,* **Market Rap: The Odyssey of a Still-Struggling Commodity Trader**, *I wrote the following as part of the introduction: "If you're one of the lucky intuitive few who can bypass the lonely and difficult path I've outlined, I imagine you'll discover your gift relatively quickly." John Baca is the guy I was envisioning—living proof that some, albeit not many among us, do possess elusive talents bordering on the paranormal.*

*John gets in synch with markets as effortlessly as Mr. Spock mind melds with alien life forms. A self-described "feel trader," he spent years in the financial pits; spreading various interest rate futures against each other. His primary focus was the MOB—muni bonds verses 30-year T bonds.*

*He'd trade large, but differently than a lot of "size" traders. Most of his biggest positions were the result of gradual "scaling"—adding more as the market went his way.*

*"I never felt comfortable fading the market" John said in reference to the practice of adding to losers or "cannonballing." "I liked trading momentum."*

*During my ill-fated year of attempting to master muni bond pit trading, I stood near John, shooting the bull with him one second, and getting out of his way the next, as he'd hit a broker's fifty-lot order. Inevitably, he'd then yell over at his clerk in the adjoining bond pit to get him into an opposite position. He wouldn't get the edge on the second side, nor did he need it. He was his own built-in advantage, a veritable trading machine who could switch into action mode instantaneously.*

*Except for occasional flashes of an intimidating temper, John remains soft-spoken and unassuming. He was a source of conjecture even among the relatively small group that stood around him; despite daily personal interactions, people would speculate about him as if he were the Wizard of Oz. How much has he actually made? What drives him? What's his story anyway?*

*He lives in an opulent yet tasteful 10,000 square foot palace designed by famed architect George Washington Maher. It's an official Chicago historical site, recently showcased in Chicago magazine. John's wife, Karen, has considerable designer expertise, and John's no slouch on the subject either. He animatedly discussed why he prefers Maher's works to that of his more famous onetime associate, Frank Lloyd Wright.*

*I met with him in his office in the Board of Trade building. He rarely trades on the floor anymore, bowing to, among other factors, tighter, more efficient markets and increased competition within the pits. ("I went from making money 90 percent of my days to maybe 50 or 60 percent.")*

*It took him a couple of years to make the transition from the diverse pit frenzy (for which he confesses a lingering yearning—screen trading gets lonely) to cold numbers on a monitor. His intuition proved to extend beyond determining which traders are sweating the most, or which clearing firms have the biggest commitment; with the aid of some technical tools, he is now efficiently "feeling" the markets surge or hesitate across cyberspace.*

*I'm in awe of John Baca (as this fawning text no doubt betrays). He's not just a model of inspiration, but accessible and likeable as well. Both the information I was learning about him for the first time and the characteristically succinct, rational way he conveyed it were further evidence of a self-assured man in control. There was almost none of the excess I've had to occasionally wade through in other interviews —what follows here is almost the result of turning on the tape and plopping its contents intact onto the page.*

*On the other hand, John's story is obviously more a counterpoint than an affirmation or commiseration of the main theme of this book—the universal experience of the life-altering Mega-Loss. Most traders stand on a precarious creaky ledge at some time in their careers. The best (or worst) that John could offer was a handful of experiences where he was out a lot of money—though never a career-threatening amount—and he was nervous and his stomach knotted. But although the ledge may have been shaky, there was always a safety net underneath. John just wouldn't play it any other way.*

---

"I knew from really early on I was going to make it," John Baca said. "It goes back to when I was a kid. I grew up in a rough (Chicago) neighborhood in a difficult family. From that, I developed instincts that helped me make decisions."

He was fanatical about games and sports, including baseball, tennis and hockey. He excelled at chess to the point where he was competing in state tournaments. Typical of John, he would use the "psyche-out" as part of his competitive arsenal. One of his unnerved conquests angrily flung the board across the room.

John even had occasional opportunity to square off against such masters as Karpov, Reshevsky and Spasky.

"Chess really helped me develop competitive strategies," he said. "I would kind of feel out my opponent, or feel out this or that, and if I got an instinct right away, I would go with it. If I didn't, I'd sort of play along until I did." (Obviously, a helpful trait years later when he'd patiently await market opportunities).

In a business in which traders typically go through thousands of dollars before finding their legs, John was never down more than $500. Very early in his career, he was up about $1000, and still trading one and two lots when his innate sense assured him he'd found a home. What's unusual about his epiphany was that it sprung out of a fluke trade.

"In the last minute (of the trading session), I gave a broker a market (bid and offer prices) in the back month. He said, 'alright, I'll buy ten.' I was just starting out, I believed in starting slow, so I said, 'no, I'll sell you two.' Then he grabs my tie because I was going to run over and try and buy two in the top month and therefore have the spread on and he goes, 'alright, I'll buy eight at'—and he bids a tick higher. So I sell him two more," John laughed, "and he kept doing this sort of thing, higher and higher, until he got all ten.

"So it's in the last minute, and I had to run across the pit to the spot (front) month broker. I was panicking because now the back month was bid higher and I was short ten, and I didn't think I'd be able to spread it off at a decent price, or even get it off at all— there was like 15 seconds. So," John further cracked up over the memory, "I hurtled myself over two guys, and I'm trying to get to the broker and I'm trying to buy evens." (A price ending in an even point increment with no thirty-second fractions— 9700....9800).

"He had an order to sell on the close, so he yells 'sell it at even!' and he runs down the steps, 'sell it at 31! SELL IT AT 30!' And I'm trying to buy evens from him, and I finally get to him, and I'm grabbing him but he doesn't want six lots, he needs to sell fifties and hundreds. So he's pushing me out of the way and I'm grabbing him and there's spit flying everywhere, it was disgusting!" (More laughter).

"I ended up buying...two at 30, two at 29, and six at 28. I made like $2,500. I was shaking for about 15 minutes after the close."

His recent prior job had been working on the loading docks. To make $2,500 in a matter of seconds struck John as unreal, but re-doable.

"That's when I knew I was going to make it."

His sixth sense works in other ways as well.

"This might sound corny, but I can hear the truth in someone's voice. When meeting someone, I could tell right away if I could trust them. It really seems to be more than just a first impression."

This connection sometimes manifests in unexpected ways. I used to be surprised in my pit days when John would, for example, ask for my opinion of the S&Ps. Why would he want my opinion? Why would he want anybody's?

One day, I knew that he had put on a losing S&P short based on what I had said, and I knew that he had been irritated, (he hates to lose in anything) but I figured his needling me was a goof as in, ha ha you idiot, why did I listen to you? Only during the interview did I discover how much he had taken my words to heart.

"I was going to kill you!" John told me. "I'd had a good day in the bonds, the notes, the munis-I had made like $12,000. All day long, I knew I was losing in the S&Ps, but I really wasn't paying attention to what the increments were worth. I think I had like three on, and I totaled it up at the end of the day, and it was like, 'holy s---!' I'd lost all my money back, and then some!"

Another time, a one sentence rejoinder from a female trader, "oh, this market is going lower," prompted him to reverse a position.

"She was a technician. I didn't necessarily listen to her all the time, although I respected her opinion. But I remember this one time in particular, because I was long, and she got me short, and I made a lot of money. It wasn't what she was telling me. I just understood the truth in her voice."

John Baca is certainly unique to the point where one wonders if his experiences are relatable at all. What can he impart about losses? Plenty, if you consider both what you can and cannot take away with you.

"I can remember being scared a handful of times," John admitted. "One of them was a day some number came out." I can't remember what the report was, but it was a terrible day. It knocked the market down a couple points."

John often reacts as a market hesitates. He was short bonds, and once they stopped roiling over the report, he began buying munis.

"I thought I was buying at a point where there was a good relationship to where the bonds were. I bought, and then bought some more to where I had about 150 on. Then all of a sudden, I think it was a big stop order being hit—they started tanking the munis. They knocked them down a half point, and I bought some more. Then they knocked them down some more.

"I was short the bonds on the other side, but the bonds had stopped moving down, so this thing was really in my face. I ended up with over 400 muni longs, which is really a lot of munis to have on." (Even years ago, it wasn't a very liquid market).

"It scared me. At one point, I was down $150,000 to $200,000. It would have never tapped me out, but it would have been a significant loss had I just panicked and gotten out. I waited and it came back so I wound up losing not all that much."

You hear this a lot from big traders—the idea that markets tend to drift back to more optimal exit points. (Floor legend Tom Baldwin has also espoused that strategy). Yet neophyte traders have the opposite drummed into them—take your losses quickly, don't let them feast on you. John can't offer an exact method for sorting out the two ideas. To him, it gets back to that intangible trader instinct.

"There's really a fine line between a good trader and a bad trader," said John. "When it could cost you your job, your livelihood, how should you respond? For that, you could ask a hundred different traders and get a hundred different answers.

"How do you know when to get out? When you're saying, 'Geez, all I want to do is get out so I can breathe again' you're starting to see the light at the end of the tunnel. Everyone has their own comfort level. When you start sweating, you've got to realize there's a problem.

"I guess the main thing I do is, I approach my exits the same way I do my entries. I scale out. And every time I take more off, I realize that I'm able to breathe a little better."

Another idiosyncratic thing John does to let some steam out of the pressure cooker is to buy himself something on bad losing days.

"Nothing big...not a car. I'd just go buy myself a nice tie or a nice pair of shoes to make me feel better.

"And I'd let it go. I wouldn't bring it home with me. Win or lose, I'd look toward the next day."

Usually. Once in a while, however, his emotions would get the better of him. It wasn't necessarily during his biggest losses; but rather on days when he did something he considered stupid.

"Stupid, as in trying to fight the market, which is not what I'm good at. But some days, I'd keep selling it higher; fighting it, thinking it's got to come back. That isn't necessarily true.

"It'd keep going against me...I'd get out finally, I'd go home...and I'd be furious with myself. I always like finding the trend and going with it, and here I am fighting it, and getting spanked."

So to blow off steam, he'd go into the basement and slap hockey pucks into the wall. "There's a few holes down there," he laughed.

For the most part though, John just keeps moving forward, pretty much the way he always has. He likes where he is now far better than where he's been, and that's probably what drives him more than anything else.

"I never have enough on to jeopardize being on the floor. Because I love the game. I've made a living off the game, and I respect the market a great deal.

"Once again, I just trust my instincts."

# *Tim York*

## Chapter 17

# Tim York

## "I WAS LIKE A ZOMBIE THINKING 'WHAT IN THE HELL JUST HAPPENED'?"

*Tim York holds big positions and assumes big risks. He wins big and then spends big— loses big and then suffers big. Then he wins some more. He is like a raw nerve—reactive to market and outside stimuli in a way that all traders are, to some degree or another. Tim's emotional makeup, however, seems especially hyper-attuned.*

*His destiny never seemed to point anywhere except toward agriculture. He managed his father's farm, and in young adulthood, purchased the first of several he would own. His particular dream, however, was to enter the commodity field, which he did in 1978. He became a broker for Heinold commodities in southern Illinois. Soon after, he moved to another company in Nashville, Tennessee and spent five years increasing his customer base and personal assets. Then, one of his clients, a wealthy surgeon, outlined a vision of his own.*

*"He wanted to place a person in Chicago," said Tim. "He offered to buy me a seat and provide enough for us to trade balls-to-the-wall."*

*Obviously, there would be no way to embark on such a venture and simultaneously hang onto his "book" (client list). In what would prove to be far from the last time of his life, Tim decided to roll the dice.*

*By the time it became obvious that the doctor was a bit of a flake, it was too late for Tim to re-route. He had already turned his clients over to other brokers, and had readied his family for the move to Chicago. At that point, the surgeon was offering an alternate plan—Tim could rejoin him in southern Illinois, and the two would run a new makeshift brokerage house. With his bridges burned, Tim didn't see any other choice.*

*"Within a month, I knew I had made a bad trade," conceded Tim. "I asked him, 'am I going to Chicago or not,' and the guy said 'uh-uh'."*

*This aroused the maverick in Tim, (a common trader characteristic). Someone was telling him he couldn't, so Tim became determined he would.*

*Thus, in 1983, Tim embarked on his trading career at the Mid America Commodity Exchange. After a short time, he felt he wasn't succeeding to his satisfaction. He took a job as a changer phone operator, a service that bridges Midam contracts to matching ones in the big primary markets. Members use it to lay off big orders that their own pits can't accommodate, or to take advantage of price differences between two exchanges. The Midam had some huge fence-swinging locals in those days, including the legendary Richard Dennis. Tim was handling a consistent, heavy flow of orders, which helped him get comfortable with the concept of trading "size."*

*Then the changer company went out of business but again, Tim didn't have to face an uncertain future for long. He answered a newspaper ad for a company called First Financial Options Group. The firm trained him and provided him with a trading stake in return for a profit percentage. Tim's dream was now a reality—he had a trading career at the CBOT. His skills caught the attention of Bill Ossmann, a large soybean oil and meal trader, who set Tim up in another proprietary arrangement.*

*In quick succession, two major events impacted Tim's life. His nineteen-year marriage ended, and the grain markets went wild.*

*1988 was a major drought year, a time of tremendous opportunity. Tim, pushing his high-risk envelope to new extremes, didn't fail to capitalize mightily.*

*"I knew how to trade 'up' markets, and I knew how to hold onto positions," he said.*

*In what would become a recurring pattern, Tim's first phenomenal wave of success was quickly followed by a crisis period. As has been frequently recounted, one's environment beyond the pits can affect trading performance, and Tim had entered an unhappy three-year second marriage. As it was ending, his career almost went out with it—he was in debt and searching for work in non-market sectors.*

*Once the divorce was finalized however, ("and the clutter was out of my life"), Tim was able to rebound in characteristically quick fashion. Trading for himself and owning a seat for the first time (the CBOT's COM gave him floor rights to all options at the exchange), Tim continued to work the grains into a hot hand, more or less until his major setback in 1996.*

---

1993 was a topsy-turvy year for grains. Whereas rain usually is as much a friend to shorts as heat and dryness benefit longs, 93 was a flood year. It was heavy rain that drove November beans to a high of $7.57 1/2 per bushel, and a couple days of sunshine that caused the customary sharp retracement.

It was a great year for Tim York, and the two that followed weren't bad either.

"I proceeded to buy more farms, more motorcycles...more things I thought made me happy," he recounted. "I had done so well in the fall of 95 that in the beginning of 96 that I thought I'd like to trade on a yellow badge." (He was referring to the full membership badge—the only one that allows floor access to CBOT grain futures pits).

He leased a seat, went into the corn pit, and discovered that he was comfortably fielding size orders. During one memorable January day, Tim recognized that he had become "one of the boys," as he caught big up and down swings in the corn pit following a crop report. The broker kept feeding him large block trades. At one time, Tim was holding three million bushels.

There was a point during the day where he had been down about $80,000, although he didn't realize it during the session. Like a unerring sleepwalker, Tim was in the plus column by the close.

"The best trading days I ever had were days when I was totally lost," he confessed.

In the calm of off-market hours, he snapped back to the realization that he was less vulnerable in his familiar options pit, where he knew the variety of ways to spread off losses. His prudence wasn't enough to avoid a universal phenomenon, however, namely that one is most susceptible to big losses when one is flying the highest.

The stage for Tim's mishap was set in early 1996, when a complicated situation known as "hedge to arrive" was occurring in corn elevators. It involved farmers selling to elevator operators with the intent to sell more as the price continued to rise. It was a speculative play, although the farmers were hedging by buying in the futures market. Contracts specific to the practice were entered by both sides, which resulted in a weird margin loop—operators would get a notice, but were able to satisfy it by taking ever more delivery. The situation kept feeding on itself, driving corn higher and higher until it had exceeded the unprecedented $5.00 level.

Once again, Tim was in his element.

"I got on this one, and I parlayed it. By the time mid-May rolled around, I was up more money than I had ever seen in my entire life, and I still had the position on as well."

Tim has had a history of trying to press his luck in outside markets as his fortunes grew in his own pit. The results normally haven't been good.

"I decided that wheat would have to go up, just like corn did. I ended up acquiring a position of about 200,000 bushels of wheat as it proceeded to go down. I adopted this kind of casualness. I began to get a laissez-faire way of thinking 'it can't get me'."

More than once, he has done nothing to stop a relentless hemorrhage simply because he couldn't feel the pain of loss. As the sun washes out visible starlight, Tim's pit success numbed his awareness of how monstrous his other losses were becoming

"Then it does reach a level where it starts bothering you. When it got to the $200,000 point, I began thinking I would never throw $200,000 at any single market in my entire life, and yet that's just what I'd been doing here."

"Clutter" was starting to encroach his life again. Single at the time, he was in serious relationships with two women from different age groups—and getting stressed over his inability to choose between them.

"I eventually decided to dump the wheat, and dump the younger girl, keep the corn...and I headed to Sturgis, South Dakota with the other girl for the vacation of my life. We played and we partied, and we played and we partied some more for two weeks.

"I came back on Sunday night, August 12, I believe. A grain report came out in which the USDA decided to factor in an early frost, something they had never done in the history of their entire existence. They dropped their yields, and created a bullish scenario which caused the corn to open locked limit up."

Tim had not lightened up during his vacation. He held a mountain of options spreads with a bearish bias. They were so positioned that not only would he lose money as the futures rose, he would also, in effect be increasing the size of his net short holdings.

"It was the worst thing you could have on when the market was limit up," Tim surmised.

Although the locked futures weren't trading, there was still maneuverability in the options.

"We started trading 18, 20, 22, 24, 29, 30, 33 about as fast as I just said it, and synthetically they were trading about 33 cents higher than where they had closed." (The corn futures limit is twelve cents).

"Some guys went ahead and started trading, because the edges in the market were humongous. Strikes that had been trading an eighth the Friday before were trading for six cents."

Tim couldn't take advantage of the situation. "I was shell shocked," he said. "I was like a zombie thinking, 'what in the hell has just happened'?"

It kept getting worse.

"I ran my position and found out that I was short the equivalent of 189 futures contracts. By then, we were trading (synthetically) 33 cents higher.

"When it was all said and done, I decided that this was too significant a move for me to be able to hold on to and say, 'hey, I'm right'."

So unlike past experiences, Tim just bit the bullet and offset the entire net short part of his position. He bought 189 synthetics, which neutralized his projected exposure.

He pegged his loss at $389,000. He felt like everything he had worked for during the year was gone.

"I saw everything flash before me...my farms, my fun times, my motorcycles... all gone."

He was in fact still up for the year, and painting a somewhat darker picture than what the situation warranted. The shock was humongous, though, and sudden. Besides, he'd also had the earlier wheat loss to exacerbate his mental decent.

In a daze, he walked upstairs to his clearing firm. The officials had been monitoring all their members' trades throughout the day—not unusual in times of turmoil. One of them came up to Tim and assured him he'd done the right thing. Tim asked him what he meant, and the man replied, "you got out."

In Tim's mind, there hadn't been much of a choice. "I wanted to be able to sleep that night."

He has since rebounded—2000 was a very good year for him, but the incident still haunts him. He is now considering imminent early retirement, although he admitted that he's overdramatized such scenarios before. If he does follow through, he conceded that the loss will have been a factor in hastening the move.

On the other hand, Tim's parachute will be golden enough. He has already reached the level of where he doesn't have to worry about curtailing what he deems important. He now owns two farms, having recently sold a third. He's been devoted to his girlfriend, Theresa, since working through his '96 emotional morass. He goes to motorcycle rallies and has aspirations of buying a bar.

That's where his balance lies these days. He's already seen the kind of mountaintops that only a high risk long-ball hitter can. Trading has been a passion for him, but only one of several. At 52, he's still young enough and determined enough to enjoy life—on his own terms, as always.

~

*Don Sliter*

# CHAPTER 18

## DON SLITER

## "I WOULD MAKE MONEY FOR FOUR DAYS, AND THEN ON THE FIFTH DAY, I WOULD BLOW EVERYTHING."

*S&P trading phenomenon Don Sliter comes across as young, vibrant, and casual. He spends most of his time these days in his spacious office in the South tower of the Chicago Mercantile Exchange. He greeted me in Adidas jogging pants and a baseball cap bearing his company logo, "Slidog."*

*He initially declared himself a poor candidate for the book because he's more of a "plugger"—one who takes quick, consistent profits and rarely goes far into a trading hole. "I'm extremely disciplined," he said.*

*In probing a little further, however, I discovered that such hadn't always been the case. There was a two year time frame at the Board of Trade when he had been more or less a loose cannon; another example of how a trading legend often emerges Phoenix-like out of near annihilation.*

*He launched his market career at the Board of Trade in 1978. He started as a runner for Prudential-Basche and then moved to Refco. The period, lasting four years, involved only outside customer business. Don didn't get any floor trader interaction until 1982, when he started working for Shatkin.*

*At that point, he became hooked. He loved everything he saw—the autonomy, the hours, and the potential huge money commensurate with trading life. He knew he wanted in.*

*"I've always been good with numbers," he said. "You find your one niche in life, and fortunately this was it."*

*He leased a seat in 1984 and traded soybeans for six months. Then he moved to the Board's equity contract of the time, the Major Market Index, (also known as the maxis or MMI). This involved a near-waterloo; probably more punishing overall than most accounts in this book. In contrast to the quick hit and recovery most subjects have recounted, Don consistently floundered during his two year stint in the maxis.*

*He underwent a major internal shift as a result of having to temporarily resume his clerking life. ("That was painful.") Once he regrouped, with the financial help of a fellow trader, Don began his stellar S&P career at the Mercantile Exchange, from which he has never looked back.*

*"I leased a seat and had a lousy spot in the pit. Fortunately, it got busy."*

*Overnight, his vantage point dramatically improved after the 1987 crash thinned out the ranks of locals.*

*"I got the best seat in the house," he said. "Right on the rail, business right behind me. No pushing or shoving—I'm right on the bumper."*

*He became at one time, by his own admission, the biggest trader in the S&P futures pit. He'd handle up to five hundred cars when contracts were worth twice their current value of $250 per full point. (In other words, with his mega-position, a one-point move altered his equity by plus or minus $250,000).*

*In 1998, he began easing his way from the floor into his upstairs office. Was it a personal preference or more a response to the changing market environment?*

*"It was time," he said, adding only that trading errors had been becoming a problem. He traded so large and frantically that he'd frequently fail to record the opposing trader's badge. "The cost of doing business is huge with me."*

*He still spends about 25 percent of his workweek in the pit. The rest of the time, he tends to his business, Slico Clearing Firm, which accommodates 50 traders. He also oversees an arbitration division that targets takeover stocks, and he is also committed to financially backing traders.*

*He enthusiastically described the website he's in the process of constructing.*

*"It'll be different than most. We'll put our money where our mouth is. We will not do anything or make any call without executing the trades ourselves.*

*"The trading will be live on the Internet. We'll add entertainment—I've got quite of few characters working for me who will be good on camera."*

*And, of course, even off the floor, he trades for himself. (In addition to S&Ps, he'll get into Nasdaq futures, bonds, and individual stocks).*

*"I pick a point to get in, one to get out, and a stop point. Then I turn off my screens. Watching them only makes me do stupid stuff."*

*He meant it too. I was hoping to track my hapless S&P short while I was sitting there, but none of his many screens had it up.*

*It was just as well. It enabled us both to do our jobs better.*

---

"I would make money for four days, and then on the fifth day, I would blow everything. I was self-destructive."

Don Sliter was talking about his days in the now defunct Major Market Index (MMI) pit, a time that must seem like a long-ago, far-away era.

"I'd make five, six, eight, ten, and then lose forty. Total lack of discipline."

Part of Don's problem stemmed from alcohol abuse. He sidestepped AA, ("I don't believe in it"), but did receive counseling. He learned that his indulgent behavior was rooted in other issues. For a significant period, he totally abstained from alcohol. In the last few years, perhaps consistent with some programs that claim a success rate with moderate drinking, he'll imbibe minimally now. ("Not even enough to where you'd call it social drinking," he said, "maybe a beer or two.")

Aside from the large losing days capsizing his steady progress, Don's dark period was defined by other counterproductive activities.

"I'd overtrade, for one thing. When I was down, I'd press, which is the stupidest thing. I'd set no limits.

"A lot of times, I would spread the MMI and the bonds. Instead of just taking my loss, I'd try to get out in the bonds, which was really ridiculous because, as you learn later, they're supposed to go opposite."

His spiral reached a climax in September 1986, during expiration. He had a mind-numbing 275 contracts on.

"I lost seventy or eighty thousand in the course of minutes," he recalled. "I had no money, I had to go back to work. I was in debt."

Returning to his clerical duties at Shatkin was a humbling experience.

"Of course!" He scoffed when asked if he'd felt devastated. "It was my life. I had nothing else to do."

He had serious doubts about whether he'd be able to make it after all. He even toyed with the idea of moving out of town. Luckily, a fellow Maxi trader recognized potential beneath Don's kamikaze veneer. Bruce Williams, (today a soybean giant), lent him money and encouraged him to start aiming for singles rather than homeruns.

Don remains grateful to this day, and remembers Bruce as being the only supportive trader at the time. His sole other emotional foundation was his wife, Marilynn.

"She said if I stopped partying, I'd have a chance," recalled Don. "She stuck by me the whole time. I've been married for nineteen years—I've been with her for twenty-three. That was hell in the mid-eighties, believe me. She was paying the rent out of her paycheck because I'd go blow it.

"She stuck by me. That had to be really, really tough."

Fortified by his two boosters, and his own belief in himself, Don promptly leased a seat at the Merc and headed for the S&P pit. "I knew it was my last shot," he said.

Come hell or high water, he was going to avoid ever having to be an employee again. Being on the high wire though, without steady income, was especially intimidating this go-around. Somehow, the fear and resolve combined to propel Don into the upper echelon trading realm. He began enjoying a consistent return that bordered on the superhuman.

"Up until last year, March, when I broke my ribs, I never had a losing month," he said. "We're talking like 14 years." Not even his transition to primarily screen trade threw him, although Don admitted that it was a bit of an adjustment. Even that hurdle is apparently behind him, though—he enjoyed his best year ever in 2000.

"I took four months off—the whole summer," he said with the near glee of a truant child. "I coached baseball. Coached the all-stars, coached everything—I enjoyed it." (He has two children—a daughter, twelve, and a nine-year-old son).

He spoke several times about how often he'd get away—during the course of a year, or even within a workday. For Don, the method has proven to be more than an indulgence—working only during smart, optimal time periods has actually boosted his bottom line. At one point, he started referring to another trader's "better work ethic"—but then he corrected himself.

"I'd do things different," he summarized. "I'd work the morning, and then I'd go play basketball for two hours and then work the afternoon. It worked better for me, so I can't say it was a bad work ethic. When I'd come back in the afternoon, I'd feel exhilarated and everyone else was—" (He slumped his shoulders for effect).

"I was starting to get migraines by 1991. The doc said, 'go relieve stress in the middle of the day.' It worked."

Don isn't about to join the harried millennial masses in the near future either. Anything work-related is going to have to take its place in line behind what's really important to him—family, peace of mind...

"I want my kids to grow up in one place," he said. "My daughter was two when we last moved, so she doesn't remember. My son has never lived anywhere else.

"I moved like eight times when I was a kid. I want my kids to grow up in that same house."

Even his retirement plans center on a kind of pastoral serenity. He hopes to open a camp for younger children—a place where they can flourish and learn.

"Coaching, traveling, baseball...that's my life right now," he mused. "Trading isn't my life anymore."

# *Chuck Wafer*

# Chapter 19

## Chuck Wafer

### "He said I should get myself back to Chicago."

*Ask Chuck Wafer what defines a good trader, and he'll invoke a word that tends to make other industry people squeamish.*

*"When I first came to the floor, almost everyone down there was a gambler," said Chuck. "They'd all be betting on gin, golf, and going to Vegas 20 times a year. I was always a gambler—I'd bet football, basketball, I'd play cards..."*

*He thinks today's breed is different. Many of the money manager types, systems players, etc. don't arrive with a riverboat mentality. Still, even they wind up wagering in the market. In Chuck's view, the word embodies the kind of risk-taking inherent in the business—nothing to get apologetic over.*

*As an indulger in the demon G-activity myself, I've marveled over outlandish trader-gambling legends recounted in books and on the trading floor. Here finally was an actual first-person source.*

*"We went to Soldier Field one time," said Chuck. "One of the guys, Tom Trankina, was upset because somebody had missed a field goal. He said anybody could kick a forty-yard field goal.*

*"Pretty soon, we had about a hundred guys on the field with Trankina. He got three tries to make the forty yarder, and everybody was betting all kinds of money."*

*The result—Trankina and Chuck both won their bets. There hadn't been a doubt in Chuck's mind. "I knew the guy."*

*He was also a non-participating eyewitness for the more famous story centering on former Bears quarterback Bobby Douglas. This bet, staged at the old Comiskey Park, was whether or not Douglas could peg a softball from home plate into the left field seats. (The legend, getting foggier with time, has it that, for pride's sake, he accomplished the task right after having lost the bet during the official trial).*

*Except for some harrowing reversals, Chuck Wafer has enjoyed success throughout every phase of his market career. He began trading futures in 1970, and four years later was working at the Board of Trade for Hornblower, an established stock brokerage house that was just starting a futures division. Chuck managed their floor activity, providing trading recommendations over the in-house squawk box. He was given a seat, which he used jointly for his Hornblower duties and his personal trading in the soybean pit.*

*Throughout most of the seventies, the grain markets provided wild opportunity. Chuck's trading quickly became sizeable enough that his job became a liability. He'd be dealing in outtrades or other clerical errors while holding gigantic, ever-shifting positions.*

*"I'd lose more (from market positions) in a day messing around with their problems than they'd be paying me in salary for the whole year." Not unreasonably, he bid farewell to Hornblower, and bought his own seat.*

*Chuck remained on the floor through 1991. Toward the end of that period, as the markets lost some luster, he'd find himself trading outside the pit about every other day. He decided since his success was no longer hinging on floor access, he might as well relocate to where "there was warmer weather and a better atmosphere." He moved to San Diego and began his life as a screen trader.*

*For years, the changeover had "no bearing" on his performance. Lately, though, he's had to settle for diminished results.*

*"The game has definitely changed," he conceded. "I have no edge. But I don't think today it's any better on the floor."*

*His other professional activities include stock investing and venture capital funding. (He is part of a group that sponsors startup businesses). Also, as he has done for most of his life, he invests in real estate. Like others in similarly volatile livelihoods, Chuck rests easier when his fortunes are converted into hard assets.*

---

Whether due to his natural ability, the friendly market environment, or a combination of the two, Chuck Wafer's trading career hit the ground on a run.

"In the first six to nine months, I was telling people it was like taking candy from a baby," he remembered. "I said I didn't know where I'd been my whole life...why I hadn't gotten here sooner."

His first rude awakening hit quickly, (and typically, at the end of heady successes).

"I got caught on the wrong side when beans locked limit down," he said. "I lost everything I'd made in six months and then some. I owed money to my clearing firm."

Typical of the freewheeling era, Chuck had no trouble borrowing money from another trader, a man who hardly knew him. The only slight connection was that the lender was doing brokerage work for Chuck's former company, Hornblower.

"He gave me $20,000," said Chuck. "I told him I had nothing in the way of security to give him and he said 'don't worry about it.' When he wrote me the check, he had to ask how to spell my last name."

That got Chuck back on his feet. He soon repaid his lender and his clearing firm.

Years later, he further squared his obligation when his former benefactor hit hard times. Chuck suspected the guy wasn't particularly reliable, but wouldn't consider not lending him the $20,000 he was requesting. Chuck wrote the check; accurately assuming he'd never see the money again.

In 1979, he took his kids on a Florida vacation while leaving yet another sizeable bean long open.

"I was trading very well and making good money. It was their spring break , so I went down with them to a second home I owned at the time."

During Chuck's absence, beans abruptly reversed direction and locked limit down.

"A couple of days later, the guy from my clearing house called and told me I didn't have any business being on vacation. He said I should get back to Chicago and take care of business."

By the time Chuck returned home, he was down $1,500,000 on the trade, and owed $700,000 to his clearing firm. He was worth that much in real estate assets, which the official agreed he need not liquidate.

"He allowed me to just day trade," said Chuck, "no overnight positions. I think it took me about two months day trading to pay back the $700,000."

By way of understatement he added, "We had good markets at the time."

Although the former two incidents depict Chuck speculating on infrequently-realized damaged-crop scenarios, he is, for the most part, skeptical of dramatic bean rallies.

"We always end up with decent weather, and we always get the crop planted," he observed. "Every year, the fools always pretend like we're not going to get it planted, and every year, we do."

He had such an opinion at the start of 1988's big drought year. As dry weather hit during the early spring and prices crept steadily upward, Chuck shorted a ton of futures. He also, for good measure, wrote (sold) a boatload of call options.

"I just felt it (the price advance) was overdone. There hadn't been any damage yet.

"Then the market took off, and at one point, I was down three and a half million dollars."

He had $1,500,000 to give his firm, which left him two million short. This time, the man in charge was Chucks personal friend.

"We went to lunch that weekend and he said, 'hey Chuck, I believe in your position, I believe bla bla bla, and don't worry about it, I'll back you all the way.' Monday morning, it was up nearly limit again. He came to me in a panic and said, 'hey, I want you out of your position!'

"What could I do? I was trading with his money all of a sudden.

"I went in and covered about half of it. I told him I wasn't going to cover any more, that I just had a terrible feeling that this was the top of the market. And he said OK."

The market closed lower. It then locked limit down for the next three trading sessions.

"I made enough to pay him back the two million, plus a little more. I would have been able to get it all back had I stayed in the whole position."

For rather apparent reasons, Chuck was known on the floor as "The Iceman." "I was trading limit positions," he said. "Nobody knew if I was long or short. My expression never changed."

There was, however, more to Chuck than what his professional poker face was betraying.

"At one point, when I was down the three and a half million, I thought I was going to have to sell my house, liquidate all my apartments, liquidate everything. It was tough. I'd be up pacing in the middle of the night, trying to figure out what I was going to do, how I was going to survive.

"I didn't hide anything—my family knew. I had a son in business school. He called me and was worried about what was going on. It was a real struggle."

Chuck prevailed. His story was yet another case of self-confidence bordering on the surreal. That his faith was consistently rewarded is a testimonial to how a gambling mentality is best accompanied by a degree of skill.

Presumably, his most extreme chance-taking days are behind him as the trading landscape changes. He lists a few reasons why the glory days of grain volatility are gone for good. Brazil's sudden prominence is a big mitigating factor.

"They can open 160 million new acres to plant whatever they want at some point. Within a couple years, they'll take over (soybean-growing) leadership."

The Freedom to Farm Act is a second damper. It sets $5.26 per bushel as a minimum floor level that participating farmers be paid. (As of this writing, the commodity is in the mid-four dollar range). It's more prudent to plant beans than, say, corn, which the government is pegging at $1.85 per bushel.

This policy is in direct contrast to the old "Payment-in-Kind" program, in which farmers were reimbursed to idle land. There was always the chance for fireworks when resulting shortages would combine with unanticipated weather problems.

Finally, today's option strategies keep a lid on volatility since they present so many additional strategies for complex hedging. As a result, you rarely see a limit day, according to Chuck.

He doesn't agree with those predicting an imminent end to floor trading, however.

"I still think the floor is the most efficient facilitator of trade," he said. "With some other markets, like bonds, maybe they'll move it more in the screen direction, like they've already been doing for years.

"With grains, though, I think we'd lose an awful lot of liquidity and a lot of players if they went strictly online."

In other words, the world in which Chuck Wafer flourished won't disappear soon. He'd bank on it.

*Joe DiNapoli*

# Chapter 20

## Joe DiNapoli

## "I Wasn't Going to Be the Wealthiest Guy in the Graveyard."

*Joe DiNapoli is the president of Coast Investment Software, Inc. The Sarasota, Florida-based company offers Stand Alone as well as CQG and Trade Station 2000i compatible software that allows subscribers to automatically access all of Joe's preprogrammed studies.*

*Joe has been trading for over 30 years. His technical approach incorporates many of the well-known leading and lagging indicators, including displaced moving averages, stochastics, as well as a variety of oscillators. He is probably best known for his work with Fibonacci numbers. His most recent book,* ***Trading DiNapoli Levels*** *is, in part, a comprehensive study of the popular retracement-related integers.*

*His company also offers hands-on educational services and materials to its followers, with Joe personally contributing via online instruction, or through small seminars held in his trading room. He is also a prominent figure on the lecture circuit. His name topped the list of whom readers of "Technical Traders Bulletin" most wanted to see interviewed according to the publisher, Chuck LeBeau.*

---

Not every trader is compatible with the theme of this book; notable losses of significant personal impact. Losses themselves are inescapable, of course, but large life-altering ones are not always a given. The floor trading population, for example, contains a relatively high percentage of people who have been "grinders" throughout their professional careers. They endured learning curves, but because pure scalping was always their goal, they were never in an open position long enough to get into significant trouble.

Joe DiNapoli wasn't the only trader to politely balk at the prospect of contributing. "I don't mean to sound above it all," he responded in an email, "but I have never had a trading disaster."

As it turns out, however, market life has taken Joe DiNapoli to the brink in a way not unlike blowing through a personal account. Stress can be present well before someone is pushed to the financial wall—even when underlying causes aren't readily apparent.

Joe's entire career has been predicated on mitigating such pressures. Early on, he gained respect for money management and leverage. He was taught frugality from his thrifty mother. His father instilled in him the idea that money was power—something not to be squandered. Furthermore, if you wanted to have fun with money, you could gamble, but "speculation was a business with rules and forethought."

In the late 1960's, Joe was trading cheap over-the-counter stocks on money borrowed from his credit union. He became infatuated with the concept of leverage; of what percentages of overall capital could be committed to given trades. He developed crude mathematical models around the concept. He began netting consistent gains through the tried-and-true method of cutting losses, and letting profits run, although he admitted to leaving significant money on the table. Pushing winners to the limit was never his big forte.

Still, he was successful as he first turned his attention to the futures market in 1980. He started trading 30-year T-bonds.

"I opened an account with a tiny amount of money," he said, "because I knew it was highly leveraged and a different game than what I was used to. It took me about six months to lose about half the account which, while being an insignificant monetary loss, damaged my ego somewhat.

"I'd told myself the account was for learning and that I could sustain such a loss without being bothered, but in my heart, I'd thought I'd make a whole bunch of money right away. That wasn't the case. It convinced me that my methods needed to be spruced up, and that's when I started to get heavily into technical analysis."

The task was far more daunting 20 years ago than now. Computer price updates were not yet commonplace. Joe remembers listening to the old price boards clattering away while he struggled to keep his five-minute charts updated by hand.

"That wasn't going to make it," he concluded.

He has historically regarded his challenges as "problem-solutions." The problem was that he needed to get profitable in this new arena. The solution was he needed better tools.

"I got a few books, and did three years worth of research on displaced moving averages and oscillators. I ended up with a CQG TG 20-20—a very powerful machine at the time. I souped-up my methods quite a lot."

He went on to invent "the oscillator predictor" in 1982, which positively impacted his winners.

"I wanted to take profits consistently," he said. "I like to cut my losses short, but I like to cut my profits short too! There are ways of finding logical places in the market to take profits, and as time went on, I improved on that. I also improved my entry and exit techniques greatly with the introduction on Fibonacci analysis."

As a result, Joe found himself within the relatively rare company of consistently successful futures traders. Furthermore, he achieved the status without ever having to endure the emotional toll of the Mega Loss. His disciplined money management approach, effective trading techniques, and deeply imbedded fiscal attitudes kept him financially grounded. Everything directly trading-related was under control.

Unfortunately, Joe was about to get blindsided anyway by a less-readily apparent market aspect.

"I had been trading the S&P since it first came out, and by approximately 1986, I was a very, very aggressive short-term trader," said Joe. "I was actively trading S&Ps off a five minute chart, constantly in and out of them during the day off of predefined Fibonacci levels.

"I was also day trading bonds and the Swiss Franc. At the time, I was also looking at perhaps fifteen other commodities on a daily basis. I'd hold overnight positions in those, while continuing to make intraday trades in the other three markets."

He lived on the west coast at the time, which meant dealing with early market hours; (5:20 a.m. for interest rate and currency futures). As an admittedly morning-adverse person, Joe would set his alarm for 4 a.m. ("It takes me a while to get up.")

That didn't mean he was about to skimp on his normal California life-style.

"My trading room overlooked Hunnington Beach," he said. "I don't know where you'd get a better night life."

For years, Joe burned the candle at both ends, partying until midnight and rising four hours later. He shouldered all this on top of the usual market pressures.

"I thought I was indestructible," he said. Consistent with frequent depictions of Life Before the Fall. "There was nothing in particular that made me feel anything was about to happen."

One unremarkable morning, Joe got up, had his coffee, did his yoga and dragged himself into his trading room. Business as usual.

"I had an overnight Swiss Franc position, which was doing just fine. I had a bond position that was profitable, and I'd just added to it. The stock market opened at 6:30, and 20 minutes later, I was holding a significant S&P position. All three of my positions were doing well.

"I felt tired, but that was normal—it was early. I was looking at the screen—one of those little 13 inch green monitors—thinking how smart I was."

Something started going wrong with his vision. The beige figures against the green chart backgrounds appeared to be dissolving.

"I started feeling light-headed and a little bit nauseous. I couldn't figure out what was going on. I got up and walked outside my trading room, opened the door and stood in the fresh air. The sun was coming up. I took some deep breaths and said, 'Jesus, what the hell was *that'?"*

The symptoms passed, and Joe returned to his station, feeling that the weird event, whatever it was, was now behind him. Then it happened again, worse than before.

"I couldn't read anything on the screen," said Joe. "I went to the quote page, and couldn't see that. The monitor was unreadable, but I knew there was nothing wrong with it."

Joe described the image as sort of like frosting melting off the side of a hot cake. As panic welled inside him, he called up and closed out all his positions. Even that would prove daunting, as he couldn't read his writing to double-check his holdings in his order book. He went outside again for more air, and then back inside to lie on his bed. He couldn't understand why the bed was shaking, until he realized that it was actually his pounding heart. He broke out in a cold sweat, and wrapped himself in blankets. He'd immediately get hot, and then cold the instant he removed the covers.

He feared he was going to die. He remembers getting his first flashes of insight—what did the number of zeros behind your net worth really mean anyway? Certainly, the game wasn't worth *this.*

After two hours elapsed, he conceded that he needed help. He managed to get dressed and precariously drive himself to a nearby health clinic.

He was given a stress test, which revealed no heart problems. The doctor concluded that Joe was having an anxiety attack, which, not surprisingly, he traced to the pressures of his livelihood.

"Your body's telling you that you need to relax," said the doctor. "You're trading too much."

"That's when I had my epiphany," said Joe. "The bottom line was, I was squandering my health and well-being for the next tick in the S&P."

The financial returns weren't worth it. Neither were the accolades Joe would hear every time he called in an order. The personnel on the other end would treat him like a guru—showering him with praise, asking him where he got his fabulous numbers and often shadowing his trades.

Joe wondered why that was important to him—he wasn't, after all, like other ostentatious traders projecting a grandiose lifestyle. He lived fairly modestly.

Suddenly the glory seemed stupid and pointless. Even the money began to feel far less important.

"I made a decision to significantly change my life," said Joe. "I wasn't going to be the wealthiest guy in the graveyard."

So Joe delved back into his internal problem-solution guidebook and concluded that the first thing that had to go was his over-committed position size.

"Instead of looking at 15 to 20 commodities, I began looking at only two—bonds and S&P. I only traded the S&P."

Interestingly, once he started doing that, his spoo account doubled within six weeks. All his extra activity had been deceptive, like meaningless "noise" within markets.

"I didn't have to sacrifice money in order to deal with my stress."

Because his main focus was now intraday market activity, he no longer had to sweat overnight positions. He didn't have to be present for market openings, which allowed him to banish his alarm clock.

"I would wake up naturally and go into the trading room," he said. "If I missed trades, I missed them. I didn't care."

Then he did something that allowed himself to sleep later still.

"I moved from the west coast, where the (S&P) market starts at 6:30, to the east coast. That was a huge benefit for me. I stopped burning the midnight oil. I controlled my life so that I got sleep. That was one of the single most important things."

He made the filters on his entry signals more stringent.

"Instead of actively trading every possible move, I would wait for big Fib numbers and major patterns to show up."

Again, Joe found to his amazement that the scaling back had little to no adverse effect on his bottom line.

"I could make as much money and work a tenth the amount. Now during certain times of the year, I'd stop trading altogether—like during summers, and around Thanksgiving.

"I had always used money management. Now I was using personal management, and that's what optimized my trading."

It was an obvious variation of the old saw "work smart, not hard." Joe quickly incorporated his added knowledge into his existing lectures. His interaction with traders undergoing similar trauma produced some interesting anecdotes. A doctor, for example, knew that he wasn't handling intra day trading well. He confirmed his suspicions after hooking himself up to various bodily function measuring devices.

When he saw what he was going through physically, he got off trading short term. He said that if he'd kept it up, it would have killed him. He went back to trading smaller size of daily and weekly charts.

In another example, a woman, who became an effective trader and money manager under Joe's tutelage, maintained her equilibrium in a unique way.

"After the market closed, she would go into her shower and scream at the top of her lungs for at least ten minutes. It worked for her," he deadpanned, "but I'm glad I wasn't her landlord."

Apparently, it wasn't a completely successful treatment though. As with Joe, she eventually had to take time off and reassess.

Joe radiates enthusiasm as he recounts what his lightening up process has brought him.

"This event, scary as it was, was the catalyst to become involved in the training and software I offer today. I've met tons of nice people. I've traveled around the world half a dozen times. There are so many things I've been able to do in my position as a trader and a teacher. I could do just as well monetarily, and enjoy life a whole lot more."

He's determined to never let his old habits re-emerge. Whenever stress threatens to undermine him, he consults with a trusted advisor.

"Every day now before I trade, I ask the manager part of myself if I'm capable of trading. One of the ways he decides is, before I go into my trading room, I go into my bathroom and look in my mirror. Do I have black around my eyes? Do I look tired and weary? The trading manager part of me asks a very simple question. 'Would I trust this guy with my money?'

"If not.... he's not trading today."

# David Gray

# Chapter 21

## David Gray

## "It Didn't Feel Devastating."

*It's possible that David Gray's biggest break arose from his own insecurity. In 1984, he was an MBA student at the Chicago Business School—one of the youngest members of his class.*

*"I was 22 when everyone else was 26 years old," he remembered. "They'd all been out in the world, working at New York Bank or whatever, and were now getting sent back for their MBAs. They knew how the world worked, and there I was, trying to pass myself off as something that I wasn't. I'd go to interviews and didn't know how to talk the talk, or walk the walk, or dress or anything."*

*For a course in street savvy, David went to the Chicago Board of Trade. He hoped to become a runner and continue his schooling. Both plans were scrapped when floor legend Ray Cahnman offered him a trading stake.*

*"I don't know what he recognized in me, but whatever it was, I'll be eternally grateful," said David.*

*He traded on his mentor's outlay, and in return gave him a share of the profits. Some would regard David's situation as a can't-lose excuse to go for broke. They'd reason that by swinging for the fence, they'd either hit it big, or walk away no worse for wear, only to leave their sponsor holding the bag. (Some actually have launched phenomenal careers doing just that).*

*David, however, sized up his situation differently—this was a potentially great career opportunity, not a lottery shot. He steadily earned money for Ray Cahnman, and within a half year, the veteran encouraged him to strike out on his own.*

*David knew that he wanted to be an interest rate spreader. He recognized early on that he was more in tune with which contracts were strong relative to others than he was with overall market direction. He pondered where to launch his solo career.*

*"I'm five foot ten, and was about 165 pounds then," said David. "I knew I had no business going into the (30 year) bond pit."*

*That left the Ginnie Maes—the only other active interest rate contract at the time. Unlike other traders, however, David wasn't about to make a permanent home anywhere.*

*"I never wanted to stand in a pit that just trades the front month," said David. "I've never wanted to trade just one contract. I've always gone to wherever you can trade multiple things."*

*The burgeoning interest rate sector continued to add new contracts, and David traded them all. He'd leave a dwindling pit for a more promising one, and have no qualms about going back again, and maybe back and forth several more times. His spreading covered the gamut, from calendar—one month against another within the same market—to inter-market. He'd appear wherever he'd perceive opportunity.*

*The loss David recounts would strike most people as sizeable. That it was harrowing but not career threatening is a testimonial to how well he was doing by the age of 25.*

*Because he was so adept at recognizing floor opportunity, he was ultimately forced to acknowledge advancing storm clouds. The most adverse change, from his perspective, was the precipitous drop in T bond volume.*

*As a result, in the summer of 2000, the ever-adaptable David joined the growing ranks of screen traders. It took him only four months to adjust to the transition.*

---

Three years into his career as a floor trader, David Gray hit his first major wall. It occurred on October 19, 1987, Black Monday, and he obviously had a lot of company.

"The markets had had some wild days," said David. "We'd had the Mexico crisis. When Greenspan replaced Paul Volker as Fed chairman, that moved the market."

At the time, the S&Ps were hovering in the mid 200s. Daily ranges never hit 10 points, and there were no trading limits. Save for a sudden dramatic range expansion in the week just before the crash, there wasn't a lot in equities to suggest an impending crisis.

Bonds, on the other hand, had been volatile the whole year. The two point daily limit of the time had been hit nearly a dozen times. (You almost never see similar movement today).

"Markets were out of control a lot," said David, "and commensurate with that, incomes were up."

That included his own, of course, but typically, David strove to remain emotionally grounded. Unfortunately, he was not flat (position-less) on the fateful day. Considering his net worth and what had been seen in the markets to date, it was far from an irresponsible decision. The anomaly of Black Monday, however, suddenly made everyone seem over-exposed. David came in long the maxi equity futures, and endured an unprecedented 29-point down opening gap.

"I got long more, and realized something was wrong," said David. "The Dow was down 100 points, but it wasn't coming back. I got out and went back to work trading credit markets."

The closed out maxi loss cost roughly $60,000.

"Both bonds and stocks continued to go down together. It felt terribly bearish, so I put on an extremely bearish (spread) in the municipal market."

The possibility of a fund exodus into the bonds didn't occur to David. "We had never seen what we now call 'flight to quality'." (Panicking investors withdraw from stocks and funnel it into safer interest rate instruments, thus driving financials sharply higher in inverse proportionate to the equities drop).

He held the position into the close. "That night, I was sitting home with my wife and the stock market had crashed. I called up to see what was going on with the bonds, and they told me the bonds were limit up."

They remained frozen the next morning on the opening—no trade. Spreads were not locked, however, so David unwound his positions. That cost him another $100,000, or $160,000 total counting the previous day's maxi loss.

"Terrible Tuesday," the day after the more famous Monday, has been reputed to have brought us closer to the brink than the actual crash day. It seemed to David that the world was coming to an end.

"I had the clearing firm write a check for all the money I had left, and I put it in my pocket. Nothing was trading; they'd basically shut down the stock market. Only the maxis remained open, and that rescued the market." (The maxis rallied sharply in the time frame that the S&P futures were closed down. That day's low became the ultimate bottom).

David then decided that the apocalypse hadn't happened after all, unless you were talking about his personal experience. After picking himself up and brushing himself off, he realized something.

"It didn't feel devastating. I was a 25 year old guy who had dropped well in excess of $100,000, and yet I had had days were I had been much more devastated losing three, four, five thousand dollars.

"I felt like *one thing* had happened. I still feel that way today; if I lose huge on one trade, I don't feel like I've become a bad trader. It's that I've made *a* bad decision, but that I can still trade.

"The days that really get to me are the days where every trade is wrong, but not necessarily huge. Days where you just get nicked and nicked and cut and nicked. At the end of the day, you walk home and you're down—whatever—$5000, $10,000. It's not the end of the world, but you feel devastated because everything you did was wrong."

David has had other opportunities to test his single-trade-debacle-theory. In the most recent example, he was long crude oil the day Clinton released the petroleum reserve. So far, his conviction hasn't wavered in the face of new onslaughts. Days where David, as he puts it, "steps on a land mine," merely demonstrate "a bad trade, not a bad trader." **

---

** I must say, despite being exposed to constant trader philosophizing, this idea was both new to me, and thought provoking. As a system developer, I try to remove "outliers"—extreme anomalies—from my data. (Or at least discount their historical significance). Why would it never have occurred to me to apply the same standards to myself—my personal involvement in the market? It's amazing that David could grasp this in the middle of a siege...at the tender age of 25, no less.

It seems eerie how quickly skilled traders can reverse their misfortune just by keeping their cool under fire.

"The following day, the markets had come off limit, so I was able to trade in a frenzy," said David. "I was focused. I stuck to the things I knew how to do. I went from my worst day ever to my best day ever, and I got the whole $160,000 back by the end of the week. It opened my eyes to possibilities of what a big day could be, both up and down."

In fact, he had an even bigger up day in December of that year. When it became evident that a recession would not result from Black Monday, David put on the same bearish interest rate spreads that had spanked him before. In a sense, he had been right all along, save for the brief disruption of the crash.

"I think I have more big down days now than most people do, but they're the result of singular trades going bad. I make money on a daily basis, and then I get blown up on a single trade. Instead of letting that eat at me, I just come back in and get back to work.

"When it's a series of nicks, when every trade seems to be wrong, then I think I'm the worst trader in the world. I go home, I don't talk to my wife and kids. I plop myself in front of the TV like an idiot and get angry.

"When I have a big losing day, it's usually because of one bad trade, and that doesn't bother me."

Like any trader looking to improve, he seeks ways to identify the land mines ahead of time. Sometimes there are permanent lessons for him; (he has a sign above his computer telling him not to short the equities on the last day of the month). Often, the misfortunes merely represent an unforeseeable downside that makes his particular normally successful trading style possible.

The gains are going to be slower and steadier, the losses are going to be larger but far less frequent, and at the end of the whole cycle, David figures to be standing.

Normally when he commiserates with his wife about career mishaps, it's to assure her, "I'm not messing with the grocery money."

# Tom Willis

## CHAPTER 22

# TOM WILLIS

## "I HAD MY APPROACH DOWN TO WHERE IT WAS ALMOST LIKE A BATTING AVERAGE."

*It seemed fitting that one week after the Chicago Board of Trade announced it was shutting down the Mid America (Midam) Commodity Exchange, I was interviewing Tom Willis. Much of the trader's lore centers on how effectively he made its small, relatively illiquid markets work for him some three decades ago.*

*It was called the Open Board of Trade back then, and was, as it had been for over a century, an independent entity. It was purchased by the Board of Trade in 1986, and operated out of a separate room on the exchange floor. Full members had access to all its markets, and for part of its fifteen years as a Board subsidiary, the Midam chugged along respectably.*

*That was before online trading, increased worldwide competition, and ever tighter, more efficient markets would challenge the supremacy of commodity exchanges. As seat prices tumbled in Chicago and elsewhere, and as exchange business leaked to a multitude of new trading arenas, the Midam lost its ability to support itself. The Board, enduring financial woes all its own, decided it no longer wanted the added liability.*

*Several eventual trading giants got their start at the Midam. It provided scaled-down versions of contracts listed on the bigger exchanges. Novices could suffer their near-inevitable learning curves by taking losses in smaller markets. Their startup costs were also minuscule relative to the primary floors.*

*Trading life was never unfamiliar to Tom. His uncle, Charlie Burbulis, was a prominent egg and pork belly speculator at the Chicago Mercantile Exchange. Tom worked for him for a couple of summers, but didn't see a realistic possibility of becoming a local himself.*

*"I knew I wanted to get in the business, but I came from a fairly modest background," he said. "My family didn't have the sort of money to buy memberships."*

*His eyes were opened to another alternative, however. A* Chicago Daily News *article profiled a young trader named Richard Dennis, who was knocking them dead at the Open Board of Trade. Tom not only had his imagination fired by the eventual legend, but suddenly he was cognizant of a market entryway he could afford. On his twenty first birthday, he paid $1000 for a membership.*

*The floor was small and run-down. Old, dilapidated curtains covered the windows.*

*Nothing was about to dampen Tom's enthusiasm, however; not even the fact that he felt compelled to continue his less exciting education at Valparaiso University, Valparaiso, Indiana. He wasn't sure yet that his new trading endeavor would be enough to fall back on, and he admitted to having little in the way of assets; ("no job, no money, no family connections....")*

*Beside, he needed the college deferment to avoid the Vietnam War. (He discontinued as the war was winding down and his financial hamstrings seemed less overwhelming, although he noted with pride that he did go back and get his degree in 1989).*

*Besides himself, Richard Dennis was the only other early 20-something in the pits. "We became friends," said Tom, "and he became instrumental in helping me formulate my early thoughts about how markets work."*

*Rich introduced Tom to relative market strength, a key methodology of Howard Malman. Traders utilizing the concept are looking to be outright buyers or sellers, not spreaders. When they do want to buy, they'll select contracts within related sectors or a complex that are most apparently rallying or holding their ground. Conversely, they'll sell the lagging markets.*

*Tom didn't have to scramble much to maneuver in the grains—they all traded in the same pit. Similarly, gold and silver, both thriving in the mid to late 70s, were also accessible. Tom didn't stop there though.*

*"My philosophy was to take as many trades with a perceived edge as I could," he said, "so I wound up trading pretty much everything that was listed. Individual markets at the Midam were never deep enough to sustain a big living for someone standing in one contract month, or even in an entire complex. Since I didn't have depth in the markets, I increased my breadth. I created latitude by spreading off my risks in unconventional ways.*

*"To me, an edge is an edge is an edge. I never cared where I got it. I think it's fair to say I probably had a bid and offer up in every second of every day."*

*Within four years of his arrival, Tom's combined scalping, position trading and relative strength techniques, (plus, whatever else he could use to secure an edge) produced enough for a full Board of Trade membership. Despite the fact that he could now trade the liquid markets in more textbook fashion, Tom continued to research, refine and apply the same strategies that had made him a Midam success.*

*"After four or five years of my ten year span as a floor trader, I had my approach down to where it was almost like a batting average," he said. "My expectation in coming to work was that I would win three times, lose once, and break even one time on a weekly basis."*

*He kept careful track of how many ticks he'd make or lose. Eventually, he decided that, much as he stood to learn from such disciplined tallying; it wasn't prudent to be so engaged while market opportunities were flashing in front of him. In response, he devised a mathematical formula that served as a kind of business plan.*

*"I took the number of trades I'd make in a day times the average edge in the pit—that being the difference between the bid and offer. I'd divide that by two, because half the time the participants were right, and half the time they were wrong. The number I arrived at, plus or minus ten percent, was very close to what my statement would say the very next morning."*

*He became wealthy and eminent enough that by the early eighties, people were clamoring for him to manage money. (Particularly people who traded on the floor with him). In 1982, he recruited his boyhood friend, Bob Jenkins, to become a partner in one of the first and only commodity trading funds of the time. For much of its initial five-year history, Willis-Jenkins, Inc. was at, or near the top of the performance ratings.*

*It was closed in 1988. When it reopened in the mid-nineties, it continued to produce high returns, but eventually, lost enough of its members that the partners again discontinued it in 2000. Highflying dot-com fever era may have contributed to the exodus. Although Tom has taken his share of notable losses, his two fund-management experiences may well have caused the most significant personal impact.*

Tom Willis doesn't seem to follow the usual pattern of adversity being a pre-requisite to growth. He got out of the pits years before floor traders would find themselves struggling relentlessly harder for ever-diminishing returns. He did so in the middle of a flourishing career; largely as a result of one incident that convinced him there was ominous writing on the wall.

It was 1979, and the Hunt brothers were just starting their ill-fated bid to corner silver—a play that would spike the metal through $40 an ounce before it would ultimately crash and languish in a prolonged bear phase. Even at this early point in the move, however, the market was carving out historic highs.

"It was volatile," said Tom. "It wasn't unusual then to get fifty cent to dollar ranges."

According to Tom, the dynamic of the era was vastly different than today. Two major groups dominated the futures markets. The commercials, or end users of products, such as grain processors, commanded information that existed beyond the pits. They had most of the money.

The locals got what remained, including the immediacy of being in the middle of a thriving order flow. Because "paper" (outside orders) was constantly being funneled in from both the buy and sell sides, traders had no trouble getting in and out...many, many times. It was a scalper's paradise.

The hapless masses keeping the money machine going were the retail customers. They paid high commissions. They routinely accepted bid-offer spreads that were relatively wide and inefficient. They had no live online prices or charts...no keystroke-accessible information. They routinely, according to Tom, "made very bad trading decisions."

Tom's self-described defining moment occurred one day when he found himself squaring off with an outsider who was proving to not be the usual pushover.

"The customer bought five hundred (Midam) silver contracts near the high of the day, early in the day. This when it was trading at around $16."

Tom estimated that he had personally covered between 50 and 75 contracts of the large order, making him short. Holding so much in such a wild market was nerve-wracking, but at least he felt he was on the right side. The customer play represented what was then historically a bad move, and sure enough, he was losing.

"As the close approaches," said Tom, "I'm thinking 'this guy is going to come back and take his loss' because that was the style at that time. We're talking about a guy who was probably out fifty cents on five hundred Midam contracts. So he's out a quarter of a million dollars on a day trade. I'm expecting him to come back and get me out, get himself out, and come back to play another day."

The closing bell rang with no sign of the trader. That a non-commercial interest would take such a loss home was almost unheard-of at the time. It led Tom to wonder, "well, just who *is* this animal out there?"

The next day, the market opened plus fifteen cents, and rallied to a 75-cent higher close. The mysterious masked man was now a winner, and he was still hanging on.

He turned out to be a fund manager, which explained the apparent lack of fear. He was merely conducting business on behalf of many clients. Suddenly, the game didn't seem so routine.

"It was really a new feel," Tom recalled. "With a little bit of snooping around, I found out that it was just a fund that maybe consisted of five hundred $25,000-$50,000 accounts. When the market was down $500 a contract into the close, a guy with a $50,000 contract was out one percent. Not a good trade, to be sure, but not the end of the world. Not even close."

And that's when it dawned on him that the mix he was used to was slowly shifting. The commercials and locals would no longer hold a monopoly, and the people entering orders were no longer going to be predictable and easily manipulated. There was a new kid in town, and Tom intuited he was going to be dangerous.

"The local became the low man on the totem pole," observed Tom. "He was the least capitalized. He's the one with little or no game plan.

"Floor traders were suddenly being asked to take the big risk at the wrong time. They'd make very little if they were right, and lose a lot if they were wrong. That's a very bad equation for success."

Tom reasoned he could make trading decisions that were at least better than the manager who had provoked him. In a variation on "if you can't beat 'em, join 'em," he and Bob Jenkins launched Willis-Jenkins, Inc.

The fund incorporated Tom's successful floor techniques. By now, his approach was pretty much contained within one all-encompassing system. The prospectus, however, allowed for system overrides and other discretionary activity. This enabled the partners to incorporate non-system considerations, such as floor dynamics, imminent reports, etc. With such savvy mavens at the helm, that could prove a definite boom, but could also backfire as Tom discovered during drawdowns. People would wonder if the wide-open approach meant chaos—a wild roller coaster ride, which Tom denies.

"We were discretionary traders, and we promoted ourselves as such. We had a systematic approach to generate signals, but we had the discretion to override them.

"For about five and a half years, we kind of knocked the cover off the ball. We took a NAV (net asset value) of $1000 and ran it up to $4000. I'm not sure we had a losing quarter from June of '82 to December of '86."

Then Tom got his first taste of how public expectations could diverge from what he knew to be prudent market approaches.

"We had a drawdown of seven or eight percent, and then got huge reductions and redemptions. Inadvertently, what I think we had inbred in people was that our huge returns were the norm, and that whenever we performed under that, we weren't being as good as we could be. Although we didn't create the mystique, I think there was an impression out there that people couldn't lose if they were with us.

"When we had our eight percent reduction, it meant that people ended up making only 23 percent rather than 30 percent for the year. They didn't lose, but we had significant redemptions."

The reversal largely stemmed from crude and heating oil shorts initiated in December 1986. It was an ultimately correct idea that was unfortunately implemented a bit too early.

Again, Tom was discovering that good trading decisions did not directly correlate to prudent business and public relations moves. "Let your profits run" may well be an etched-in-stone trader mantra, but outsiders have a different mind-set. If they've got it, they don't want to give it back. Unlike many managers, however, Tom and Bob were more attuned to market dynamics than the comfort zones of their clientele.

"Since we were up 25 to 30 percent on the year, we decided to risk five or ten percent in order to really explode this thing in terms of a rate of return. The trade didn't work."

The third quarter statement had revealed a year-to-date return of 30 percent. Tom imagined that a lot of upward extrapolation was being computed for December. When a drawdown resulted instead, many took a powder in search of The Next Hot Thing.

Curiously, many of the fund participants weren't exactly naive outsiders, but actual floor traders—personal acquaintances. That's what unnerved Tom the most—that people who'd figure to have a grasp of the big picture were responding like clueless pipe dreamers.

"I couldn't wait to get out," said Tom. The fund was closed, and he took a market hiatus that included finishing his undergraduate degree, and teaching a course in trading-investing.

Rested and relaxed, he returned with Bob for Round Two in 1996. They again hit the ground on a run, averaging about 18 percent returns for the first two years. But again, we're talking dot-com era.

"Most of the phone calls we'd field were of the variety of 'what's wrong with you? I can get this kind of return in one day.'"

Again, the stress the partners were experiencing was not that they were losing money for their customers, but rather, that they weren't making enough.

"It was just crazy," said Tom. "People who had given us a million bucks in 1996 walked away with a million and a half four years later."

Today, Tom trades for himself, perhaps not as aggressively as he once did. He and his wife moved to Chicago two years ago. He has five grown children, and two grandchildren. With his boyish features, few would likely guess he was in his fifties.

As with other traders who have seen their share of trading wars, Tom now hangs loose. He had recently taken a three and a half month Florida vacation. He won't rush his next opportunity, whatever it will be, but on the other hand, his thoughts never stop clicking.

"I've got a ton of ideas about what an investment vehicle in the future ought to look like—about what its goals and aspirations should be. Somebody else might be better to implement them, though.

"I'm not bitter about my experiences. I'm the first to admit, I might have seen it coming if I were a better businessman. I'm a trader, and although I wasn't inefficient or disorganized, I wouldn't confuse myself with a businessman."

I wanted a final summation from Tom on the Midam situation—the main topic of floor conversation for the week. Perhaps no trader outside of Richard Dennis would be more apropos to write an epitaph.

"I owe a lot to the Midam," Tom replied. My entry into the business wouldn't have happened without it.

"As for what's occurring now—it's a tragedy."

He wondered aloud what the exchange could have been worth to far-thinking people four years ago. It had such wide variety of contracts to offer—some that people weren't generally aware it possessed, such as mini-platinum. In the Internet-crazed time, how might it have succeeded as an all-electronic exchange—

and not a "bulletin board" as Larry Rosenberg put it—but a platform backed by the biggest exchange in the world, with safety guaranteed?

"You know why they didn't do it," he mused. "It was the usual concern—that such a move would be bad for open outcry. What would happen to all these seat holders? Well, I don't have an exact answer to that, but I can tell you this. If there had been hundreds of millions of dollars lying around, they would have definitely found a way to accommodate the out-of-work floor traders."

The gigantic amount of money that might have been commanded wasn't good enough for the Board. There had been widespread speculation, that both Tom and I had heard, that an actual lucrative offer had been rejected.

"Now they're closing it up to save a quarter million," Tom said. "All too late—all defensive moves now. And the (Midam) members will get nothing.

"They're acting like classic losers." Tom shook his head. "It's like they're making classic loser trades."

~

*Larry Pesavento*

# Chapter 23

## Larry Pesavento

## "Opinions are often wrong, but markets never are."

*Larry Pesavento is kind of like Tom Hagen in "The Godfather." He works for only one client. (He doesn't like to mention the name unless it's absolutely necessary. Joke. Actually, he trades for a large hedge fund).*

*He trades virtually any and all markets in the equities and futures universe. With his forty years of experience, Larry would be as qualified for such latitude as anyone. He trades with discretion, but within very strict trading rules from which he won't deviate. His self-imposed limitations include the following:*

> *1. For every order he places, a corresponding stoploss must be put up immediately thereafter.*
> *2. If he has a drawdown of five percent during any given week, he will quit trading for the next three weeks.*
> *3. Any position that is a loser on the third day after initiation is promptly exited on the following opening.*

*"I don't get rich, but I make a high six-figure return every year," he said.*

*He's been doing it for six years. It's a comfortable enough arrangement that he feels no need to trade his own money. He hasn't completely retreated from the general public however; you can continue to get his recommendations on his website,* ***www.tradingtutor.com.***

*He is a sought-after lecturer and author, having published eight books as of this writing. They include* ***Opening Price Principle: Best Kept Secret on Wall Street*** *and* ***Fibonacci Ratios With Pattern Recognition***

*His speculative journey began in 1959, when he was a senior in high school. He bought a small takeover candidate stock, Elastic Stopnut, and earned $400—enough money to buy a 1949 Mercury. The bug was planted.*

*After getting a masters degree in business and finance from Indiana University, he worked for 11 years in the marketing department of Eli Lilly. It was then that he began a relentless market involvement that, with rare exception, hasn't abated since.*

*"I was trading at that time—always following pork bellies or soybeans or corn or wheat."*

*His first big profit occurred in the silver market of the late sixties.*

*"The market doubled or tripled in price," he said. "I made a great deal of money percentage-wise."*

*In 1971, he began trading in the office of Conti Commodities, Westwood, California. It became a training ground for several other notable wizards, including Ed Sekoya and Mike Marcus.*

*"It was a very successful office," noted Larry. "Many millionaires were made there."*

*With the aid of the office manager, Roy Fassel, ('very talented, he's still trading to this day,") Larry developed a unique technical style that incorporated many of the well-known trading tools in unique ways. Throughout his career, he showed an adeptness for incorporating the best of what mentors had to offer; some-*

*thing easier said than done in the trading world. Among other notables who inspired him; pattern recognition specialist John Hill and Walter Bressert.*

*People would contact Larry as his fame grew in order to share ideas with him. One such woman, Dr. Ruth Miller, a former college economics professor of Larry's, purportedly demonstrated an uncanny relationship between astral cycles and Fibonacci numbers. Larry was stunned over the high returns, and chronicled the results in* ***Asto Cycles: The Trader's Viewpoint.***

*Cycle projections figured prominently in his approach leading up to one of the wildest rides of his career. It was 1972, just as the Russians were poised to initiate a staggering grain purchase.*

---

Larry Pesavento was using a cycle program in 1972 that projected 16 to 28 day bottoms in the wheat market. He was exploiting an apparently consistent ratio between the length of the cycle base and the resulting amplitude of the subsequent price rise.

Wheat was embarking on a bull run that would last through most of the seventies and become legendary among floor traders. Larry's program of buying on retracements would prove very compatible with the era. He successfully pulled it off, time after time until he had run up over a million dollars, a high water mark he reached on his birthday, July 28, 1974.

He had actually started out with a spread position—long July, short December wheat. It was a bull-friendly strategy—in rising markets, the nearby contracts tend to gain the most due to immediate demand.

Then Larry had some enormous luck complement his strategy. He just happened to leg out of his short side three days before the Soviet Union announced a major grain purchase. As the market lurched upward limit by limit, Larry had nothing on but ever increasingly valuable longs.

Flushed with triumph, and rigidly hanging onto an idea that seemed beyond reproach, Larry then entered the bear market of 1974. He lost everything and then some.

"I lost it the same way I'd made it," he said. "I was buying the cycle lows. I was trading the same way I had when I made all my money.

"Suddenly, the market was going down to its sixteen day lows, but would only rally three days and then go down again for another thirteen days. Before, it would go down three days and up sixteen.

"I was sitting there as the market kept going down, thinking it was going to rally again, but it never would. I would buy more, and just expose myself to more risk, and then when it dropped more, I'd expose myself to even more.

"Finally, I got to where I was getting margin calls and then the market would really collapse and then it'd wipe me out in a matter of a few days."

The debacle, now known as the October 1974 crash, lasted ten weeks. Larry was finally forced out of everything, and was $2,700 in debt to Conti Commodities.

"There was no CFTC (Commodity Federal Trading Commission) at that time," said Larry, "so you could trade out of a negative balance if your firm allowed you to. I traded for about two weeks to get back the $2,700. When my account got positive by a few hundred dollars, I quit trading for a little over a year and a half."

Even during his hiatus, however, Larry stayed connected to his passion. He spent considerable time reflecting on what had gone wrong and what should be done differently in the future.

"I learned three things," said Larry. "One is, you can never average a losing position. That's one of the greatest fallacies on Wall Street. People don't realize that during 1929, out of the Dow Jones' thirty stocks, seventeen went bankrupt. Buying against a losing position is always the wrong thing to do.

"The second thing is, you always have to use a stoploss. This protects you against yourself. Opinions are often wrong, but markets never are.

"Third and most important is, the only thing you can control when you're trading is risk. You never know when you're going to make a profit and you never know how much it will be. The risk-to-reward equation is what you have to focus on."

Every day, including weekends, he'd go to the investment center library. He formulated new trading strategies and re-entered the market in 1976, just in time for another runup, this time in soybeans. On this occasion, he got out near the high. His former million-dollar paper profit was now a realized asset. From there, he never looked back.

How, though, had Larry felt as he was enduring his reversal? Again, there have been many examples of traders being so immersed in doing what they perceive to be the correct thing that they don't have the time or inclination to despair. It's all they can do just to keep their eye on the ball in front of them.

"I was sad that I had made some stupid mistakes, but I was not depressed. I knew that I could get it back because I had seen other people do that. All I had to do was learn what I had done wrong. And that's primarily what I did.

"I knew that if I made the money on the way up, if I figured out what I had done wrong and turned it around, I'd probably be able to make it back. The markets were still volatile enough where I should be able to do that.

"I started with three grand, and then I lost it all. I might have lived well through the whole thing. I bought a lot of toys and stuff."

So it wasn't exactly like the coach turning back into the pumpkin.

"Nah, I was only in my thirties," he replied. "It was no big deal."

He didn't sound flip or ironic. He was coming across like the many traders who maintain that "not letting it get to you" is the only road to ultimate success.

He was married at the time. He didn't tell his wife anything about it until after their divorce.

"Hardly anybody knew what was going on with me," he said. It never bothered me because it was just money. It was nothing serious. It wasn't family or health or anything like that. It was only money, and I knew I could make it back."

Larry tends to keep his equity fluctuations to himself, but other than that, he's pretty much an open book. One wonders if maybe he's a writer before all else.

"Every time I learn something new, I like to share it with people. They like to know what I'm doing, they buy the books, they seem happy. I keep them informed. I don't have secret methods...I share everything."

He was working on a new book that should out by the time you read this, a 40-day personal trading diary. He claims he'll reveal everything he's trading, thinking, doing... It'll be a total window into Larry Pesavento.

Imagine the implications.

~

*Damon Pavlatos*

## CHAPTER 24

# DAMON PAVLATOS

## "I'VE LEARNED MORE FROM THE MISTAKES OF THE BIG TRADERS THAN I DID FROM HOW GOOD THEY WERE."

*Sometimes it's fun being a writer.*

*The three hours I spent with Damon Pavlatos at Chicago's Costas restaurant were filled with enough great food, drink, laughs and stories for three or four chapters. Damon is kind of a renaissance guy who has pretty much done it all.*

*We had a few things in common. We're both guitarists with band histories. In the seventies, Damon, fresh out of college, abandoned his CPA objectives for life on the road. He performed 170 club dates in one year. Despite his youthful stamina, the grind got to him. His brother, a clerk at the Mercantile Exchange, extended an invitation to investigate the world of commodities, and as the saying goes, Damon never looked back.*

*We're both technical traders, and we both develop our own methodologies. We share the same primary market—S&P futures. I trade it from completely off the floor, relying on 100 percent mechanical systems. Damon, by contrast, is in the center of the action.*

*In recent years, strange things have occurred in the spoos which could never be anticipated in the testing of historical data. An unannounced late afternoon interest rate cut, for example, subjected buy stop orders to an unimaginable thirty full point slippage. More recently, a half point surprise slash on April 18, 2001, catapulted the market over 50 points higher for an instant—just long enough to nail many hapless shorts. Anyone getting long on stops was then crushed in the subsequent 25 point free-fall. As an added bonus, some wretches in the e-mini S&Ps actually paid 55 FULL POINTS more than the already outrageous high in the full contract.*

*As one without access to floor dynamics, I am forced to deal with such nightmare scenarios by anticipating a big enough slippage/commission penalty beforehand—not an exact science. Damon can mitigate such problems. He initiates his trades from a CQG screen, just outside the S&P pit and can react according to what he sees happening around him.*

*We compared our mutual S&P experiences during times of historical note. We had both responded to Black Monday by pulling our money of the bank. We both wondered why no one around us seemed similarly alarmed, but we both, of course, wound up with egg on our faces. The event immediately preceded the most relentless bull market in history, and we both endured aggravation as Clueless Joe Outside Investor triumphed like an unerring sleepwalker. We commiserated over how cab drivers and dentists were touting stocks while trading professionals missed the boat entirely, (or worse, sank in a sea of short selling).*

*The first of the aforementioned interest rate cuts spooked us both, although it hadn't cost either of us money. The Gulf War was Damon's big waterloo, and unforgettable for me as well for different reasons. We remembered key events during the Pacific Rim crisis of 1998.*

*Damon will develop ideas through historical testing, but uses them more as trading tools rather than inviolate mandated strategies. His decisions are influenced by what's occurring on the floor—how liquid is it, which houses are involved, and how much is bid and offered. He can sidestep risky time frames, such as periods just before the release of key reports which, for a variety of reasons, can't be easily done by someone off the floor committed to 100 percent mechanical programs.*

*He was involved with the S&P futures since the inception of the contract. In 1982, Shearson-American Express hired him to run their floor operation, (a position he held for four years). At the time, Damon had had about five years worth of trading experience—first at the Midam, and then as a TED (T bill vs. Eurodollar) spreader at the Merc. He began a service that he continues today, that of providing a unique link between the floor and outside customers.*

*"A common mistake traders make is not understanding the nature of the market they're trading, and what it can handle. The time of day is a factor—you can do big business in the S&Ps during the first hour because that's when the big funds come in. During the 11-1 lunch time frame, you can see activity falling off in the pit. You have to know many locals are in there, what kind of volume, to move size."*

*Over the years, Damon managed floor operations for several companies and today, is a partner of the Schuler Group L.L.C. at Hammer Trading, a division of Refco Inc. As part of his routine floor operations, he'll recommend, for example, that a hundred lot order be broken into 20 lot increments in order to fill it without undue price disruptions. Conversely, he might alert someone of the potential to fill half a large order immediately by dropping the offer a tick or two. Regarding floor perils and opportunities, Damon is heads-up on behalf of his clientele.*

*Sometimes he'll do something else not exactly commonplace. He'll urge self-destructing traders to take a break. Customer orders bring him income, so obviously, the action flies in the face of his vested interest. In the long run, though, the trust he has earned is a good trade-off. Small traders who survive sometimes metamorphose into thriving large traders, and there is prudence in retaining their continued loyalty.*

*Besides, Damon is so in tune with the psychology of trader foibles that it's hard for him to not occasionally interject. (Coaxing is about as far as he can go, however—he can't exactly refuse "bad orders" without putting himself in jeopardy).*

*"I've learned more from the mistakes of the big traders than I did from how good they were," he noted. "We all basically fall off-track at times—get over our heads, add to losers, let our emotions get to us. We won't take a loss, or we'll take our aggression out on the market, which doesn't help, because the market has no feelings."*

*His rule of thumb is, if you suffer three or four losing trades in a row, back off for a while. It's a sign you're out of rhythm, and not likely to get better.*

*Because he trades for himself, he wasn't about to get out of sharing a less-than-grandiose personal trader mishap or two. Other customer-related stuff provided icing on the cake although due to his discretion, he'd only impart so much. What follows is a portion of what Damon has witnessed and/or endured throughout the years.*

---

In August 1990, Iraq invaded Kuwait. For the rest of the year, the U.S. pursued diplomacy, all the while threatening dire consequences if terms couldn't be reached. By late in the year, we had the unique specter of a "war by deadline"...President Bush (the Elder) had drawn a temporal line in the sand. If the date was reached before the Iraqis had withdrawn their troops, Iraq was assured of dire consequences.

I don't remember the exact chronology or much of the rhetoric. I recall that the S&P trade at the time was hairy even by its usual standards. The conventional wisdom was, war would pummel the market, which each new break in negotiations seemed to confirm. Once, after a failed meeting, one word uttered by then-Secretary of State George Shultz at a press conference—"regrettably"—was enough to instantly knock twelve points off the S&Ps. Obviously, there was tremendous risk in being long, but the short side would also backfire whenever something seemed remotely conciliatory.

Damon Pavlatos is unusually apologetic about his disaster-friendly positions. Most traders dismiss allegiances to droughts, pestilence and war as, "hey, I didn't create the situation." Damon sometimes seems almost conflicted.

He was once long cattle during his Midam days, and one night, while watching TV with his then-wife and mother-in-law, he caught the news of some hoof-and-mouth-like disease ravaging the herds.

"My mother-in-law didn't understand what I did for a living," he said. "She thought it was more like I was in the stock market or something. I'm sitting there going 'all-RIGHT!' and she's looking at me like I'm a sadist.

"Then I started thinking about everyone involved and it was like, 'well yeah, I do want the money, but not *this* way.' It becomes like a love-hate relationship."

Years later, during the 1991 commencement of the allied air strike one January evening, Damon experienced similar mixed feelings.

"I'm patriotic. I didn't want Americans hurt or killed."

But he was also crisis-friendly—long Deutsche Mark, long gold and short the spoos. Consistent with conventional wisdom and Edwin Starr, Damon decided that "war, HUNGH!" was good for "absolutely NOTHIN." He couldn't see being long. Furthermore, he thought his positions provided some diversity—the dollar could be weak even if the S&Ps were to rise, for example.

"It turned out that not only was I not diversified, but I had increased my leverage," he said.

At the time, there was no Globex outlet for most markets—just bad news from overseas. All three positions were moving significantly against him. He sat drinking in a bar; correctly deducing that the next morning opening was going to be grim.

He quickly took his losses in the gold and D mark. The spoos opened at their initial limit up position—then, as now, they were halted at several intraday limit levels for a few minutes before the barrier was then lifted. At the time, the volatility was nothing compared to what it is today, and five points was the first halting point. When that was removed, the market spiked to near its second twelve-point limit.

As many of the biggest traders do, Damon paused a beat before instantly surrendering. He considered cannonballing—a practice he normally avoids.

"This was one of the few times I figured I had the right to add to a loser," he said. "I was stuck, but thinking that if I weren't already in, I'd have definitely been selling."

He considered the spurt to be an overreaction—a common occurrence during times of big news. Also, his charts were indicating a huge resistance right at the second limit.

"I had to ask myself, how honest am I being about this—about what I'd actually do in the situation if I weren't already in? I knew I wasn't in my right mind. I was down almost $60,000. If I added more and it went against me (to the planned stop loss area) I'd be out $100,000 or more."

As it turned out, the market did break, and Damon's day-end loss was a very manageable $5000. "I would have been happy if it had been $20,000," he said.

The $60-$100,000 scenario would have been devastating. ("It's all relative to what I had at the time.")

Fearful he might panic, Damon purposely avoided thinking about such numbers while the crisis raged. Like other big hitters, he just focused on his task at hand.

Again, this is one scenario where, looking back, Damon excuses cannonballing. "It's sort of like you're working around an act of God."

He also acknowledged that it's necessary in situations involving size—you have to pick general areas to initiate your positions or your orders will disrupt the market. It's understandable why you'd put, say, a third of your position on at the market, a third several ticks under that, and the rest lower still. This is technically cannonballing, (or price averaging), but it's specifically planned to accommodate market logistics.

For the most part, however, most of Damon's cannonballing experiences, as a trader and a broker, tend to be negative. He told a story of how one normally good S&P customer unraveled one day.

"The guy was worth a couple hundred million," said Damon, "and he basically traded for fun. He'd trade off my opinion a lot, and one day he called me and asked me what I thought.

I said I thought the market should be sold, and that's what he thought, so we sold him ten contracts.

"The market didn't break much, and started coming back up. I gave him a level higher at which, if we traded, it would mean we were wrong. He agreed.

"We got there, but he didn't want to get out. Because he had so much money, he thought, 'ehhh, let's just sell another ten.' So we sell another ten, and he asks again what I think and I say, 'we should be long! We're wrong!' But now the guy's changing his opinion."

In the business, it's known as "defending a position;" maybe one of the biggest cardinal mistakes of all. The scenarios usually play out in similar fashion—you start out loosey-goosey because the position is small and it's just a fun thing anyway. You add to it because, since you liked selling it there, you *loved* it at this even higher price. Suddenly it's a big enough loss where it's not an afterthought any more, and you start inventing reasons not to take it. Maybe you sell still more, hoping to move up your average entry. The whole time, you're refusing to take your loss, rationalizing that it's not real as long as the position is still open.

"What happens to a lot of traders is, when a market trends, it's like inch by inch," said Damon. "If it moves up fast, it's a short-covering rally. It's not investors running it, thinking the market is going to get away from them.

"When it's a true move, it makes people think that it's trading 'heavy'." (It's going up, but laboriously so). "It's really not running away, so he's like 'hell, sell ten more!' He kept adding ten lots, from morning till the end of the day.

"At one point, when we were short sixty, seventy cars, he asked me again what I thought and I told him again we should get out. He said 'I can't take this loss. Sell another ten,' and I said 'you've *got* to be kidding!' He was getting mad...at the market, at the traders, and everybody else, all the time thinking it shouldn't be going higher. He was doing everything wrong imaginable."

All day long this went on until, finally, the trader was forced to buy back 120 contracts. Damon pegged his loss at between a hundred and fifty and two hundred thousand dollars.

That the man was normally effective echoed Damon's belief of the occasional but nearly inevitable trader foul-up. The ultimate goal could be to eliminate such missteps entirely, but you'll probably improve dramatically if you can simply keep the incidents to a minimum. (Damon estimates that he succumbs about once a month).

It's a problem traders understand intimately, even if outsiders fail to grasp it. Damon offered them a sports analogy.

"If you're a pitcher and you're striking guys out, the coach is going to leave you in. If you start walking guys, he'll pull you out. When we're trading for ourselves though.... who pulls us out when we're not doing well?"

In other words, few other arenas in life depend so much on discipline, and not just in terms of how you limit you losses and conduct your trading. The very logistics of the financial world sometimes necessitate choices. Overnight Globex activity, for example, has driven people crazy, particularly in the days when the system wouldn't take stop orders.

One night during the Pacific Rim Crisis of 1998, (during which the Eastern stock markets would routinely be down 10-20 percent or more) Damon was short the S&Ps. In sympathy with the rest of the world, they were locked limit down. Damon wanted to remain short as long as the limit held, but he knew that if they came off, the rally could be ferocious.

He planned to exit the instant they traded higher, but implementing the idea posed a problem. Again, you couldn't just put up a stop order. He was exhausted from work, which was now extending into an around-the-clock time frame, and not happy about the prospect of maybe having to stay up all night.

"Suddenly, I had no life," he mused. "At two in the morning, I'm in front of the screens with my head bobbing. I was sleepy. It had been a tough day."

He woke up a fellow-trader friend at two in the morning and said, "Look, I need your help. You've got to come here, I can't keep my eyes open."

Good friend that he was, the guy said sure. Damon asked him to sit and watch the screen—giving him careful instructions on what to do in all circumstances. Damon just wanted a catnap for an hour or so. No problem, said the friend, don't worry about it.

"So I go lay down on the couch, and I blew up my one minute chart so I could watch it from the couch," said Damon. "Then I fell asleep.

"I wake up two hours later. I look at the chart from the couch, and the market's up like 1500 points. So I think ah, s---t, he got me out. I walk over around the corner, I look at him...he's sleeping! I go 'omigod!' I look at the computer, and he had never gotten me out!

"I slapped him and yelled 'GET OUT OF THIS CHAIR'!" And he's like, 'omigod!' I'd just given back fifteen thousand dollars!"

Damon laughed heartily at the memory, (undoubtedly, something he couldn't always have done).

But the story doesn't end there.

"The same thing happened to me like it did during the Iraqi thing. I hadn't gotten out. I looked at my charts, and found a good area to put up a mental stop. I added another short" (for a total now of three). "If it traded above that, *then* I'd get out.

"When I made back the $15,000, I got out and I sent my friend home." (More laughter).

I wasn't sure about the moral here. Some traders routinely engage in cannonballing, but Damon's not one of them. He's not sure what to conclude either. He acknowledged a degree of luck.

"But, I did stop looking at the night trade," he said.

His life on the floor is full enough.

~

*Scott Slutsky*

# Chapter 25

## Scott Slutsky

# "The Market Doesn't Stop Just Because You're Stuck."

*A lot of people enter the fast track for profit, prestige—in some cases for altruistic reasons; they want to make a difference. Scott Slutsky may share some or all of those ambitions, but the characteristic he most projects is an unbridled enthusiasm that rubs off on everyone around him. Whether he's presiding over a mock trading session for an educational seminar or commiserating with a member of his staff of 85 brokers and salesmen, Scott Slutsky is...into it. He just likes it. And it seemed that over his career, the more enjoyment he was having, the higher he rose within his field.*

*He has been a member of the Chicago Mercantile Exchange for 23 years. His father was a trader in the now-defunct egg market and Scott assisted him on the floor during summer breaks and other time off from school. From his first exposure at age 15, Scott couldn't imagine any other life. ("It's in my blood," he said).*

*As computerized trading threatens to engulf open outcry, Scott can recall a time before floor prices were routinely displayed electronically.*

*"When I first started working for the exchange, I started on chalkboards," he said. "I wrote bids-offers and trades on a chalkboard for traders. They'd say 'Scott, half bid, 52 bid, 55*

*trade,' and I would have to put 'half B, 52 B, 55 trade' on the board."*

*One can find plenty of seasoned veterans who will affirm such memories, but the surprising thing about Scott is, he was only 44 years old at the time of this writing. (April, 2001).*

*After graduating college in 1979, Scott purchased a seat and traded for two years in the gold pit. Despite holding his own, he longed for the greater social interaction of brokerage. ("My personality is more public relations-oriented.") He then moved to the Swiss Franc pit and joined his father and brother in filling orders for public customers.*

*As his business rose with the then-flourishing foreign currencies, Scott's PR aspirations led him into exchange politics. In 1989, at age 30, he became one of the youngest Merc members ever to be elected to the board of directors.*

*He wrote two books,* **Masters of the Futures** *and* **The Complete Guide to Electronic Futures Trading**. *He hit the lecture circuit in 1997 and was received by a crowd of 12 people. His most recent appearance was before a Las Vegas audience of 1200.*

*"I teach educational seminars around the world," he said. "I lecture on how the trading floor works and the importance of education."*

*He hosted teachers from around the country who specialized in options, systems, charting; whatever interested the trading public. To warm up the crowd, he'd stage a mock trading session.*

*"I'd bring people from the audience up on stage with me in groups of five. I give them trading coats, badges, and orders, and I put them in a live situation."*

*He makes no bones about offering "entertainment"—a means of "providing education in a nice way." Again, some trading gurus just wanna have fun.*

*He promoted his appearances through his trade shows, conferences, and his website, Vantage Learning Center. He sold the site in January 2001, citing the difficulty of running it by himself and time away from his family.*

*His health had also been a source of recent problems. He was suffering from recurring difficulty stemming from a years-earlier procedure in which three disks had been removed from his neck. He left the floor in February, 2000. There had been no accident involved, but his steadily degenerating condition wasn't helped by the grueling rigors of the floor.*

*"It was too hard standing eight hours a day, yelling, screaming, getting pushed. So I gave that up and started trading on a Globex machine at home. I became Mr. Mom and really enjoyed the time I got to spend with my four kids."*

*His trading went pretty much the way of his prior independent venture in the gold pit some 20 years earlier. "It wasn't bad. It was a new learning experience." But again, it wasn't the person-to-person side of the industry within which he really thrived.*

*He didn't have to wait long to return to the managerial arena. He continued to acquire contacts through his scaled-back monthly lecture schedule.*

*He was soon approached by Alaron Trading Co. and is today their Director of Sales and Business Development. "The business development part was easy," he observed. "I'd already gotten to know ninety percent of the vendors in the business on a first-name basis."*

*He's in charge of 85 brokers and salespeople in four cities, including the home office, Chicago.*

*"I'm the morale officer," he said proudly. "I like people. I give them a pat on the back, I let them vent. Believe it or not, a smile goes a long way. My door is always open to them. I give them my phone numbers so they can always get hold of me. I like being one of the first ones in each morning and the last ones to leave. I love the interaction with the brokers and companies I deal with."*

---

The good thing about brokering relative to independent trading is that most of the time, you get a regular paycheck. The big downside is, you are responsible for making good on all your mistakes. It doesn't matter how much you're worth—as far as liability goes, the sky is always the theoretical limit.

Over his 23-year career, Scott Slutsky had many incidents he considered recounting. "You go to breakfast, and you notice that you have an order in your pocket that was never filled. Yeah, I've got a lot of experiences like that."

As a broker, the potential of making an error is always present. Consider the following: 10 contracts in the Swiss Franc times $12.50 per tick. The mistake is caught 20 ticks higher—if you don't buy them now, you'll risk a greater liability. That's $12.50 times 10 times 20 and you're looking at a bill for $2500.

Could be worse. Almost certainly has been, if you're a broker.

Scott finally settled on a standout event. "Yeah, I've got a good one for you," he laughed, no trace of irony.

"It was Christmas Eve, 1981. At the time, my father, my bother and I were the largest order fillers in the Swiss Franc pit. We basically controlled the order flow.

"My father and brother were not there that day. I was working alone. It was near the end of the session, and the market started creeping up higher and higher and it ran into buy stops."

Buy stops, usually used to limit losses on short positions, are guaranteed to be filled as soon as the market trades at the specified price or higher. Scott had roughly 2000 contracts that had to be executed. He didn't have the option of protesting that he ran out of time, or there weren't enough available sellers. For the right price, someone should always bite. The broker's job: make them an offer (bid) they can't refuse.

"I moved the market up 60 to 80 points by myself in increments of 10 points at a crack," he said. "I had a stack of customer orders at least six to eight inches thick."

He had a couple of assistants, and the three of them tried in vain to count the buys and sells. Scott, however, didn't have the luxury of waiting to make sure it all balanced.

"The market kept moving, so fresh orders kept coming in. I was just bidding it up blindly—half bid, sixty bid, seventy bid—just trying to buy whatever I could. The market closed at two o'clock, but by the time I had finished counting all my cards and all my orders, it was probably 3:15.

"I overbought about a hundred and fifty contracts. It was Christmas Eve and the markets were closed. There definitely wasn't any cash (currency) market that afternoon because there was no one around—everyone went home already.

"I basically had to take a position home of 150 contracts. I didn't have much of a choice."

He had an interminable three days to ponder his fate. He had trouble sleeping. As a group, traders are especially prone to taking charge of their own actions. It's one of the lures of the business, and a big reason why they tend to get especially vexed by left field surprises over which they have no control.

He returned after the holiday to a gap down opening in excess of 100 ticks. His instantaneous realized loss exceeded $200,000.

He was in his early twenties and unmarried. His chosen profession had certainly been lucrative leading up to the debacle—he was making $1.25 per contract in a market that was trading a respectable daily five-figured volume. Two hundred thousand dollars, though, eats up a lot of contracts.

"For the time, it was a great deal of money," he said, "not like nowadays where guys routinely drop that in a day. I was scared. I had the money behind me, but it was something I had worked so hard for that I hated to have that situation.

"I got out of the position and made sure everything was OK for the rest of the day. About halfway into the day, I left, went home and tried to re-group. I took a couple days off. Then I licked my wounds went back in there and believe it or not, filled orders for the next nineteen years.

"That was my first real lesson in risk management. Emotionally and physically, it was very hard."

How did his father feel about it? "Terrible, especially since my brother and him were gone on that day. Usually we have three order fillers. It's a big load for only one person to handle."

His circumstances were a little different than that of an independent trader getting spanked for a wrong decision. There wasn't much for him to reevaluate or second-guess. Still, he did take a couple things away from his experience.

"The most important thing in any situation like that is don't panic. As soon as you panic or lose your composure, you're useless.

"The second thing is risk management. Don't take more than you can handle. There's a greed factor in that every order that comes in, you want to fill it, but the object of the game is to be there for the next day."

But a broker can't refuse orders, can he?

"No, you can't refuse orders, and that's why it's very important to have someone there with you for what we call 'overflow.' That's where, when you can't handle any more, you have someone who backs you up, who will take the excess coming in. For the rest of my career, I always had a second and third person around for emergencies. They'd step up to the plate if I needed them."

I've told many brokers that I could never handle their job. It's probably the ultimate harried position. You have to be a master of thinking on your feet.

"It's hard," Scott affirmed. "It's not for everybody. I've seen order fillers come and go who have said 'oh, this is easy, I can do this.' A week later, the first time they hit a busy market, they were doubled over and hyperventilating and in tears. You name it, I've seen it.

"You know you have to fill, endorse, and return your orders the best you can. That's what you do. You don't always get the opportunity to play catch up.

"The market doesn't stop just because you're stuck."

~

*Bruce Williams*

## Chapter 26

# Bruce Williams

## "I was in sixth gear, going full throttle, and I forgot to pull back."

*Bruce Williams is the fastest talker I've interviewed. His 90 minutes of machine-gun observations filled up a cassette that was probably designed to hold a third as much information. My written pages contained chicken scratch sentence fragments. My writing hand became a cramped-up claw. Once he started rolling, all I could do was hang on for dear life.*

*Bruce is reputed by some to be the current biggest trader in the Board of Trade's soybean pit. (The description could apply to his physical presence—he's a large, rather imposing figure). He didn't see much relevance in such assessments in any case.*

*"All that's important is being your own personal best," he said.*

*For Bruce, that entails achieving membership in "the three percent club;" the trading elite that earns seven figure incomes consistently rather than sporadically. Such is the group that sleeps soundly at night, that can adjust to changing market conditions, that doesn't eventually "give it all back" as so many traders do. It includes the ones who do that extra something that others miss; the models from whom you can learn.*

*A one-time tennis pro, Bruce makes many sports-trading analogies. In both, the key to success is consistency and longevity. Traders who occasionally make gigantic quick hits sometimes illustrate a case of "nothing to lose." Bruce is more impressed with those who have been in the game for the long haul. He sees adaptability as the key to long-term survival.*

*"I've gone from headsets to arbs to the introduction of options. I've discovered how to throttle up and throttle back according to the different trading months, and how much liquidity they offer."*

*He learned over the years, for example, to scale back during the December-through- February time frame. You can't force business that isn't there. As volume starts picking up in the spring, he merely rides the tide back to his normal levels of commitment.*

*"Consistently good traders use a combination of trusting themselves, knowing their personalities and emotions, and their self-confidence. They know when to push all that forward, and when to pull it back. They adjust their rhythm, style and size. The guys who can take it from sixth to first gear, and keep it there until it's safe to shift into second or third are the ones who make consistent money year in and year out."*

*He experienced a false start a couple years before his trading life actually began. In 1980, a friend was trading at the Mercantile exchange under Ray Cahnman. Bruce and Ray had also known each other for years—as a kid; Bruce played tennis in matches that Ray sponsored. (Apparently, Ray was a good player himself).*

*At the urging of his friend, Bruce, who knew nothing about commodity trading, went to the Merc to observe Mark Burchett, in action. (Although famous for his S&P trading, Mark was working the T Bill pit at the time). The experience at any rate initially didn't inspire much in Bruce.*

*"I didn't understand a thing that was going on with the boards or the hand signals or the different colored jackets," he remembered. "To me, it was a ring of chaos. At the end of the day, I kind of patted him on the shoulder and said, 'good luck, I'm going back to the tennis club'."*

*Luckily, the trader urged him to give it another chance, and after a few more visits, "it started to click." Two years later, Bruce took advantage of a unique opportunity offered by the Board of Trade, and a stellar trading career was underway.*

---

Some of the biggest money-makers had corresponding gigantic loss stories, which they graciously supplied to this book. Others built their fortunes grinding away—through scalping, through tight money management techniques, or through an innate talent that keeps them from ever getting in over their heads. Some of them confessed almost apologetically that they simply had no standout dark trading moments to recount. Others, like Bruce Williams, had to delve far back into their history, to a time when a small five-figure loss seemed like the end of the world.

That Bruce doesn't have a tale more commensurate with his current seven-figure income doesn't diminish his contribution. Perhaps the worst trials we endure are the ones in which we're so untested and ill-prepared. Losses are a mental state, after all, and their impact is always relative.

Bruce was part of a program introduced by the Board in 1982, which was designed to get bodies into the just-launched ten-year-note pit. Obviously, exchanges have vested interest in new contracts succeeding, so during such inaugurations, unusual promotion and opportunities arise. For $1,250 a quarter, people could trade ten-year- notes on a mere permit—seat purchases or leases weren't necessary.

One hundred rookie traders signed up; many have since gone on to become industry giants. Several veterans at the time, including Ray Cahnman, served as mentors to the group. Bruce remembers learning something unique from each of them.

"Carl Boraiko stood next to me," said Bruce. "He taught us guts and discipline. Lance Murdock taught us etiquette. Rob Moore taught us speed and how to move numbers."

Finding reliable trading models is, in Bruce's opinion, crucial to a novice's survival chances. "I was able to learn from a lot of good quality guys," he said. "I was really lucky."

He was trading on a shoestring at the time—$2,000 he had saved, plus another $1,000 in borrowed funds. He was part of the group of similarly under-funded young tennis pros that Ray Cahnman had brought to the floor.

"I was totally green. It was frustrating not having a feel for it, getting picked off by the Veterans Day in and day out. It got old."

He hung in there—not doing much better as his first major shock to the system hit out of nowhere.

"The Fed chairman at the time was Paul Volker. He announced a rate hike and the market tanked."

As is typical with sudden unexpected news, the resulting move was violent and nearly instantaneous. Bruce was long about ten contracts. His over-leverage collided with his inexperience and he froze like a deer in headlights. His only split second chance would have been to lose about $1,000, but he balked, as even that seemed unthinkable. He instead remained paralyzed as the debit hole became cavernous—minus $19,000 by the time he finally took action.

His $3,000 stake was gone, and he was now $16,000 in debt— to one of his mentors, as it turned out. Ray Cahnman owned his clearing firm.

"I walked up to him about midday and said, 'we've got a problem.' He said 'just get out of it and go upstairs.' I met him after the close and he said 'write down everything you own.' That was a stereo, a TV and a couch." Bruce laughed at the memory.

"It was an embarrassing, scary situation."

For a week, Bruce was completely sidelined. Then Ray offered him the chance to assist a prominent broker, Eddie Fiala. Bruce was not allowed to trade under the arrangement. Luckily, business was booming—the Fed was intervening "nearly every day" according to Bruce, and at the end of two months, he had earned back his deficit.

He was engaged to be married in six months to Debbie, who would become his married partner and emotional rock for 20 years and counting. The couple's hopes and aspirations for the future hinged in part on Bruce's trading success. He longed to break into the inner circle, and Debbie was instrumental in supporting his dream.

"We'd talk every day, howdja do, fine, bla bla... She was really cool...she never pressured me or anything. But this time, it was a long train ride home.

"She said, 'well, how did you do today?' and I said, 'I lost.' And she said, 'how much did you lose? And I said, 'I lost everything.' And that was one of the hardest things I ever had to tell somebody."

He echoed the widespread sentiment that overall balance in life—inside and outside the pits—is crucial to success.

"You've got to have a stable home life to be a successful trader. If you're in a bad marriage, or if you've got a spouse who's not really compassionate about this business, or doesn't understand why you have to pour your heart and soul into it, it can be a total distraction from you ever being a great trader. It helps to have a good family life with kids, and also that you can separate the two.

"It's a balancing act. When you're trading, you've got to focus a hundred and ten percent on the market that you're in. When you're home, you've got to put the sword down, and focus on your family life. Put the markets away for awhile."

Traders have been known to go the Hollywood route once their success becomes spectacular.

"They suddenly don't value the spouse they grew up with. They run off with a young clerk."

Not every person has the kind of solid foundation Bruce is talking about, of course, and he's not interested in moralizing in any case. His point is that such upheaval almost inevitably has a negative impact on trading performance.

His own bad experience taught him discipline.... "cut your losses" may well be the trader Prime Directive. He wouldn't fully develop his more subtle awareness of when to press and back off, however, until after hitting the bean pit in 1988. Before that, Black Monday would serve as his second big learning experience. He was trading the Board's equity contract at the time, the major market index.

"I had my biggest day on that Black Friday. I had made deep six figures." (The session before Black Monday, the market dropped slightly more than 100 points—unprecedented for the time).

"That was followed by my biggest losing day the following Monday. I was still in sixth gear going full throttle, and I forgot to pull back. I got annihilated I wound up dropping six figures which, luckily I had earned in the previous session.

"I was a pure scalper then, and I got tangled up in the volatility...just misread the market. I had really been in tune with it, but suddenly all the indicators I was keying off on were out of line, and the tape was late. Instead of being one step ahead of the market, I was probably two steps behind. On top of that, the market got very illiquid."

The experience gave Bruce new insight into the emotional effect of windfalls verses losses. The two are not symmetrical mirror images of each other.

"The impact of a negative event stays with you longer. My big Friday was great, I was happy, but at the end of the day, I didn't feel like buying everybody beers. You just go home, and you're a husband and father again. On that Monday, though, it was a long drive home... a bigger feeling."

Losses also make for the more profound learning experiences, according to Bruce. "You build more from your mistakes."

Again, it's a balancing act—you take something positive away, but you don't let the blows consume you. Bruce today is probably incapable of freezing. There are just too many internal safeguards he has acquired over the years.

"I'll fade a trend for two or three days, but after that, my circuit breakers kick in and I'm done. I've been fighting this thing, I've lost *x* amount of dollars, and it's obviously my fault, not the market's.

"And that's the way it always is. You can blame losses on the brokers who missed you, the guys in the pit, or the market, but successful guys recognize they only have themselves.

"To be able to balance out that temperament—that's a fine line. If you can do it day in and day out, you'll be part of that three percent."

*Connie Brown*

# CHAPTER 27

## CONNIE BROWN

### "IT'S HARDER TO BE A TRADER THAN IT IS TO BE A TEST PILOT BECAUSE YOU HAVE TO LIVE WITH YOUR CONSEQUENCES."

*Connie Brown is a portfolio manager/advisor best known for her work in price projection and risk management. Her program incorporates aspects of Gann, Elliott wave, and momentum following. (Stochastic originator George Lane is one of her enthusiastic supporters).*

*The math behind her methodology can be head-spinning to the uninitiated, but a few things are clear. For one, Connie won't risk more than two percent of total account equity on any given trade, and no more than three trades, or six percent total loss, on a given trading idea. For another, her approach thrives the most in markets with a pronounced primary or counter-trend, or those in which minor trends relate to swing trading. Her nemesis is prolonged whip-saw or consolidating action.*

*"The one huge flaw to the system I work with is, when we're in a sideways market, I get chopped to death," she explained, "because I work through trading zones and price targets. When a market goes to an area that negates the original entry idea, or 'no print zone,' I immediately get out."*

*Most momentum followers get stopped out all too frequently when the market is continually shifting direction. Connie uses price projections along with momentum, but in order for her four-to-one risk-to-reward parameters to prevail, there must be sufficient liquidity to keep her mathematical pivot relationships intact.*

*She doesn't trade mechanically, meaning that her judgment is a factor, but the individual components of the program have all been determined through historical testing. She trusts the indicators, but is dubious about attempts to coordinate them into an all-encompassing judgment-free approach. ("Any system that's a black box system cannot take past experience and adjust for the type of environment that you're in.")*

*Connie has an eclectic background. Her business career began at Eastman Kodak as a sales rep, and then evolved to brand manager of the Professional Color Film Division. This provided her first link with the commodities markets, as silver is an integral part of the film process. In researching her product, she got drawn into futures markets.*

*After that 11-year stint, her next destination was Wall Street. She began in a junk bond department and was told, "Anyone who brings a chart into this trading room will be fired." Within a year, she had discovered the value of the forbidden trading tools, and her first foray onto The Street had come to an end.*

*Today, she is the president of Aerodynamic Investments Inc. She manages institutional funds in a pool structure through the company, and directly interacts with her customers.*

*She authored two trading books,* ***Aerodynamic Trading*** *and* ***Technical Analysis for the Trading Professional****, and was interviewed in "Stocks and Commodities" magazine.*

*She was at one time an Olympic-contending swimmer, which she feels helped develop her mental toughness necessary to trading. It also produced a doggedness that Connie regards as an occasional impediment.*

*"Being bull-headed contributes to what pilots call 'get-there-itis.' It is hard to take breaks to recharge your own batteries or recognize when fatigue should be respected by stepping to the sidelines of the market."*

*She's an obvious workaholic who joked with me via email that terms such as "vacation" and "tan" were pretty foreign to her. Not that she was complaining; it's apparent that her work is her passion.*

---

Connie Brown cites a conversation she had with a former test-pilot-turned-trader as one of her biggest eye openers

"He was a bright young guy—athletic, intuitive and quick-thinking on his feet—all the things that come with surviving the kind of job he had. His field was flight-testing army helicopters, which is even riskier. You don't have a lot of grace if something goes wrong.

"He described a horrific situation where his engine cut out. You literally have to fly straight into the ground, knowing you have to get as much speed and propulsion as possible. Then at the very last second, you pull up."

In the instant you pull out of the nose-dive; the gravitation slows you to the point where you hopefully survive the impact. Obviously, you only get one shot.

After the event, the pilot decided he'd do something different—something not so death-defying. Like trading.

"I was working with him because I was teaching him some aspects of risk management and price objectives. He said, 'you know, it's harder to be a trader than it is to be a test pilot because you have to live with your consequences'."

We shared a hearty laugh over that one. If you trade long enough, sooner or later, as anyone in the business will attest, you're going to have a rough flight.

Connie recently survived an ordeal in which her managed funds registered no better than fractional percentage gains or losses over an interminable year and a half. It wasn't exactly a downward spiral. It didn't even involve her personal funds, although many who have traded both for themselves and others have testified that there is more pressure in the latter.

It was an especially nerve-wracking time; the late end-of-the-century stages of the Nasdaq blowoff, when tales of outrageous windfalls were infiltrating every strata of society imaginable. "It was hard to explain to customers who were saying 'wow, look at the gains that are happening in the Nasdaq!' and you're sitting there in a market that's not going anywhere, day after day after day, month after month."

Connie couldn't put them in anything but the S&P futures. It was the agreement spelled out in her prospectus.

"From April, 1998, through the next eighteen months, the S&Ps were chopping sideways and couldn't break out of their range," she recounted. "They couldn't go anywhere. The market got thinner and thinner.

"The floor reported traders that had imploded on a weekly basis. I had never experienced eighteen months of hell and assumed the end of this marathon nightmare had to be just around the corner. The nightmare of got-to-get-there-itis became addictive. My training kicked in and I had to keep my head down, stay streamlined, and drive hard for the wall at the end of the swimming pool."

Then the insidious churn suddenly became a violent crescendo. On Friday, April 14, 2000, the Dow went into its biggest intraday decline ever— down more than 600 points before finally recovering by the close. The S&Ps went down and back through several intraday limits.

It wasn't the best time for Connie to have to do battle. Days earlier, she had arranged to take her first time off in years.

"I knew I was exhausted and needed a vacation. On the week of the fourteenth, I was packed, ready to take my horse to a dressage clinic."

An ominous fast price break on the thirteenth rattled her partners. Connie's phone rang late that night, and as usual, she found herself at work the next day. ("Pretty ticked off," she added).

She knew she had several strikes against her before the trading day had even begun. She was exhausted and angry with her partners for canceling her vacation. She had been forced to do an instant improvisation; from wind-down mode leading into vacation to full battle-readiness.

She was enduring thc pilot "gct-thcrc-it is" trap—going full speed ahead without the down time she desperately needed.

She knew that in a market meltdown, the anchor short position had to be established before the first limit-down is crossed to avoid the risk of an in-your-face market reversal. It had looked like Armageddon—eighteen months of whipsaw hell finally coming to an end. But as is often the case, appearances were deceiving.

During the interminable chop period, market conditions convinced Connie to restrict her stop limits to less than one percent. In doing so, she had negatively impacted her profit-and-loss returns. On April 14, tired and angry, she opened her stops to the maximum exposure her prospectus allowed.

"I did not want to be stopped out above the first limit-down level and then be forced to watch a developing market crash scenario from the side-lines," she explained. "You have to be positioned before the first limit is broken. Otherwise you risk the bungee cord rip of the market coming back."

Her program—spelled out in advance to the clients—was that a maximum of two percent of the total equity would be the allowable risk per trade. Three such trades on the given trading idea, or a total cap of six percent, would be the second restriction.

"What was not in the prospectus," she said, "is knowing you don't risk up to six percent when the trader is not a hundred percent."

Because she wasn't trading mechanically—her judgment was a factor—she was free to trade less than her limits whenever she determined that volatility warranted it. She had been taking such a cautious approach leading up to the market melt, which had impeded her profit/ loss ratio. The trades needed room to breathe if she were to realize her four-to-one gains.

The current decision to loosen the stops had proven as costly as her previous judgment to allow less play. In hindsight, she'd made the wrong call in both situations. The problem was, there had been no clear-cut determining factor. A trading moratorium might have been a sensible choice, but that's a luxury fund managers aren't allowed.

"You can't say 'this is a rotten period to be involved with the market, so you want to step out'," said Connie. "With money managers, that's never an option. It *should* be—there should be a smart third decision allowed where you can be off to the side doing nothing. But we have to say 'we have to find something, we're *good* enough to where we *can* find something.' People are counting on me to produce when the rest of their portfolio in other investments is in a crash. I *must* produce today.

"Wrong!"

"I was a short horizon S&P trader, living and dying through the whole period. I had the end of the month bogey where I was accountable to the clients.

"Obviously you're stressed under that situation. I wasn't sleeping well because I was also trading Germany (overnight markets) and it got to the point where my sleep patterns were so disrupted that I couldn't sleep more than a couple hours at a time. And then my eating got affected also. That should have been a huge warning flag, but I didn't recognize that this developing chain would have led to a serious mistake. The bottom line was, I lost more in two days than I had lost over the entire eighteen-months preceding the week of April 14, 2000."

It was a month later that she learned of the test-pilot analogy. Basically, experts of flight crises situations have defined three types of situations that will threaten to impact a pilot's "judgment chain" to a breaking point. Pilots can generally respond to any two of them hitting at once, but all three simultaneously becomes the proverbial camel straw.

"Here's the analogy," Connie explained. "One, you could have a flight plan where you absolutely know you're going to get to your destination, but you lose your visibility due to a heavy fog. Regardless, you know you have to get to your destination, so you press on.

"The second is where you know you're pushing through not being one hundred percent. You've been sick; you've got the flu. But you know you can handle it. You push through the discomfort.

"The third thing hits...you run into an engine problem."

Again, it has been determined that a skilled pilot has a better than even chance of surviving any two of the three together, but has only a ten percent survival rate when faced with all three.

"Obviously, this analogy applies to every trader," said Connie. "You might be able to work through not being at your physical peak, for example. But when the aircraft/market isn't accommodating you, you're sick, you're angry, you're under the gun to produce and you haven't filed your flight plan, and then on top of it, you run into engine trouble..."

Maybe all three scenarios were analogous to Connie, but it was the third one that threatened to be her career crusher. She knew her rickety S&P/ aircraft was not about to right itself.

"The NFA (National Futures Association) did a routine audit that's required for pools and said, 'you're probably one of five people left that we see that's just trading S&Ps'."

Connie knew she had to bite the bullet. She had her prospectus revised, and moved her fund into individual stocks. Now instead of having to conform to one pattern, she can select among a wide array of setups that best accommodate her.

She's grateful for her S&P experience, particularly since individual stock movement is so often acting like a futures market today.

"You learn so much trading futures. You react faster, you see patterns. You read the market in a time horizon that someone who has only traded longer horizon stock hasn't had the opportunity to develop."

Now, of course, her playing field is wider. She has more calls she can make these days, including that the next time someone wants to interrupt her vacation, she'll keep driving.

She also has a clearer picture of what to avoid; that poor judgment chain familiar to the military, for example, where compounding factors build against you and hamper your ability to function.

"Trading always comes back to discovering what stuff you're made of," said Connie. "It's not about the technical."

Dr. Michael K. Hoffman

# Chapter 28

## Dr. Michael K. Hoffman

### "I wanted to see what it was like to trade a fifty lot."

*Dr. Michael K. Hoffman Jr. heads UOT Financial Services and the University of Trading. UOT is a clearing firm. As president, Dr. Hoffman earns commissions off the traders signed up with him.*

*It's an old industry adage that losing traders ultimately aren't going to be much good to their houses. Dr. Hoffman decided that the best way to ensure they'd generate long- term consistent income was to make good traders out of them from the ground up. The University of Trading (established in 1999) is the result—a program where rookies can learn hands on, step by step, the art of pit and screen trading. It's a five level course offered over as many weeks. The target recruits are, according to Dr. Hoffman, "people committed to the idea of making a million dollars."*

*The endeavor resulted largely from Dr. Hoffman's own trading history. Prior to 1981, he was a teacher, head coach, and vice principal, having earned his doctorate in educational administration from the University of Illinois. Two trader friends enticed him to the floor of the Chicago Mercantile Exchange with the promise of wealth and adventure. More important to Dr. Hoffman was the competitive challenge. Among his several athletic credentials; college running back for the U of I.*

*His buddies were unusually generous—one gave him a seat free of charge, and the other put money in his account. They didn't, however, have much professional involvement with him thereafter. Isolated and intensely driven to educate himself, Dr. Hoffman vowed that he would someday help others in similar struggles.*

*"There were no educational courses. My friends weren't willing to sit down and talk to me about the intricacies of the business. It wasn't because they were inarticulate or couldn't communicate. They just weren't prepared to teach, and didn't understand what it was that I needed to learn.*

*"I started out in the certificates of deposit pit. I then went on to the Eurodollars, then to pork bellies. I then went to the Japanese yen, and that's where I found a home."*

*He made a respectable living there for six years, but wasn't yet excelling. "I still couldn't get to the heart of the business," he admitted, "the place of making as much as I wanted to."*

*That corner was finally turned during his next six-year stint. He became an order filler in the S&P pit a mere three months before the Crash of 87. He handled that day's deluge of orders without a problem and in fact, is the first broker I've ever heard claim to never have endured any major charge-backs resulting from errors. He attributed that in part to his practice of sending his clerks into the pit to double-check that trades were consummated.*

*"I made a commitment to be successful in that pit," he said. "That meant studying the pit, the market, and the participants. I memorized every acronym, every trader and broker's first name, and all the idiosyncrasies and trading habits of all the participants."*

*He became as adept with numbers as possible, jealously guarded his physical and emotional health, including continued commitment to his lifelong exercise regimen. He showed up for work every day, and rarely, if ever, left the pit during the nearly seven hour sessions.*

*After six successful years in the S&Ps, Dr. Hoffman, then in his fifties, was starting to feel the strain inherent in his job. He decided it was time to earnestly pursue his ultimate dream of educating traders. He took on two partners, John Oberman and Mike Mininni. They began training 378 prospective traders from which they established the startup customer base for the new clearing firm.*

*Today there are 30 active instructors in the company, plus another 20 to 30 former teachers who frequently return to contribute. All of them are themselves traders.*

*Dr. Hoffman's passion for teaching extends into the lecture circuit. As of this writing, he was preparing to host a technical trading seminar in London. He is also the author of* ***Pit Trading: Do You Have the Right Stuff?*** *Published by Traders Press, Inc.*

---

The young man stood at the office doorway looking sheepish. He'd just lost money, but one got the feeling he was more uncomfortable breaking the news to his mentor than he was experiencing the loss itself.

Dr. Michael K. Hoffman Jr. was merciful. "OK, you're done for the day. It's all right. You'll get 'em tomorrow."

In the 45 minutes I'd been sitting there, it was about the fifth time Dr. Hoffman had been interrupted either by phone or in person by excited traders reporting their progress. Every other occasion had been upbeat with the instructor responding like a proud parent praising a kid's Little League performance. What was the problem this time?

Dr. Hoffman shrugged. "I'm trying to get him to learn how to be successful, but he has his own idea. He wants to make a thousand dollars a day. Right now, I want him to make fifty."

So is the rookie doomed; a case of the wrong guy for the wrong job? "Nah," said Dr. Hoffman, "he's going to be fine. He's going to make it." "But," he admitted, "not everyone will."

Sometimes, Dr. Hoffman's job is to convince a person that their niche lies elsewhere, beyond the trading world. He'll do so without a second thought, even though it would mean giving up commissions the trader would generate. He once helped a lawyer put aside his market aspirations and rekindle enthusiasm for his existent career. Similarly, when I expressed curiosity over whether I could be taught to trade (as opposed to mechanically following systems), Dr. Hoffman's verdict was, not while I'm a writer. Commitment to the Million Dollar Club needs to be absolute and one hundred percent—second professions are a no-no.

For the remaining viable majority, the University of Trading offers an all-encompassing systematic support system. The student is coached on personal strengths and weaknesses.

"We help them come to grips with who they are as a person."

Next, the student is taught the mechanics of executing trades, (including acquiring the necessary confidence). He or she is then provided with a simple technical system. It is used in part as a tool to aid in the general understanding of how markets operate.

"We also help the individual identify what market he or she should trade," said Dr. Hoffman. "We provide them with information concerning the particular market, meaning the movement of the market as well as the types of personalities within it. It probably wouldn't be appropriate for a slow-moving individual to trade the S&Ps, for example, because they move so fast. We try to match the personality to the market. We get them to understand the market they're in through technical analysis.

"We're basically in-and-out traders. We don't hold overnight. As long as a market has volatility and movement, we believe a trader can be successful in it on a regular basis."

Every trader is given continuous support via a personal mentor-counselor. Dr. Hoffman is especially attuned to this aspect—he, after all, had to go it alone. His students, by contrast, are walked through preparatory pre-market routines and end-of-day personal performance evaluations and summaries.

It's an all-encompassing approach that includes attention to personal health and stamina. Meditation and relaxation techniques are introduced. The former athlete knows his troops have to be combat-ready.

Another thing he understands is that the war doesn't have to be fought continuously. The "more-is-better" work ethic we've all had clubbed over our heads is often counter-productive.

"Most young people want to stay and trade. They may not have anything else to do, and trading can be addictive. Having been a successful athlete, teacher and coach, I know that we get tired. The brain gets tired."

So part of the regimen is helping the traders better plan their days. Dr. Hoffman goes as far as to make a judgment on their readiness based on skin pallor, state of dress and hair, etc. Anyone not in top form can just as well spend time reading, exercising, or meditating. It's all equally valid.

This doesn't mean that traders shouldn't eat, drink, and sleep their passion, however. To illustrate what it takes to achieve ultimate goals, Dr. Hoffman spoke of the commitment level of such super-athletes as Michael Jordan.

"He'd practice before practice, during practice, and after practice. When he wasn't on the court, he'd be mentally practicing—running plays through his head."

Dr. Hoffman cited some astounding statistics regarding UOT graduates. One purportedly made between $125,000 to $250,000 in a year with only one losing day. Another made 1.4 million with ten losing days. Dr. Hoffman is quick to concede, however, that these are the people committed enough to get through the whole program, and to continue to take the necessary self-actualizing steps in their careers. It's not a given that everyone has that capacity or determination.

Dr. Hoffman, however, can usually predict odds of given success. Those most likely to excel are the ones continuously showing up to class, working with the coaches, and taking advice in the right spirit. They tend to plan a date ahead of time to launch their trading careers as opposed to those chomping at the bit to rush in immediately.

Dr. Hoffman is quite obviously a source of inspiration for them. He's one the interviewees not offering much in the way of "negative-experience-we-can-learn from." But rather, one of the fortunate few whose inner makeup allows him to move quickly beyond problem areas. He did, however, relate one occasion where he indulged his curiosity in a big way. It occurred during his time in the yen pit.

"As a new trader, I wanted to see what it was like to trade a fifty lot," said Dr. Hoffman. "It was a complete disaster, a nightmare. My timing was horrible. It was emotional. I did it because I wanted to see what being a homerun hitter was like."

He was a one and two lot trader at the time. The plunge represented for him, a one-of-a-kind impulsive move. ("The first and last time.") Luckily, he didn't compound his mistake by panicking, freezing, cannonballing, or committing any number of other common self-destructive errors. He got out quickly and took a big loss. He didn't have to sweat it overnight, though, and in fact, put a good spin on it upon later reflection.

"I did not berate myself. I was disappointed that I wasn't successful, but I was happy that I had the courage to do what I wanted to do."

"It reinforced the idea that I am who I am—a single's hitter. I had no business trying to hit the homerun."

Actually, despite a passion for the game, Dr. Hoffman was never much of a baseball player at all. A more a propos analogy might be better to related to football. Even there, he had longings that were beyond him—he would have loved to have been a quarterback.

"I was a wide receiver. It's what I was good at—what I was. I was high-strung—a sprinter. It took years for me to realize that I was too hyper to be a quarterback. A quarterback needs to be calm, cool, collected and see the whole field. That wasn't me."

It's a lesson Dr. Hoffman takes into his classes every day. The player has to fit the playing field. Market success needs to come from within and without.

"Again," said Dr. Hoffman, "it's understanding who you are."

# *John McCracken*

## Chapter 29

# John McCracken

### "The Biggest Mistake a Trader Makes Is Trying to Defend a Position."

*They're a distinctive breed, these interest rate spreaders. As with the old-guard fence-swinging grain traders, they have very defined characteristics. They consider their methodology to be relatively safe. They understand that sudden news shocks can potentially cost them a lot of money, but they accept that as part of the game. When disaster strikes, they tend to look at the bigger picture—the market volatility is providing earning opportunity. Almost to the man, the traders I spoke with were able to recoup their mega-losses in mere days or less.*

*And unlike some of the big-swinging more gambling-oriented traders, they seldom agonize. David Gray's hit "didn't feel devastating." John Baca was "scared," but knew his situation wouldn't be career-threatening.*

*Unlike those in outright longs or shorts, spreaders are always "working" something—trading around huge positions—always scaling in or out. They are the least instructional models for handling anxiety because they don't live with it long; something titanic blindsides them, they immediately immerse themselves in business-at-hand, and the crisis has lessened before they've had time to reflect. There's an old adage that speculators come and go, but spreaders are around forever. The relatively young men and women working their intermarket financial positions are a living testimonial to at least the latter half of the axiom.*

*John McCracken is another unpretentious, low-key guy who cranks out consistent, calculated profits in the interest rate sector. Over an early lunch, he revealed that trading wasn't a pipe dream to him; it was always a viable career choice, with several family members serving as forerunners. His brother worked calendar spreads in the 30-year bonds. His brother-in-law scalped outright positions in the same pit, and a few cousins traded in the grain room.*

*"I was married, and had saved some money," said John. "I didn't come down here right out of college; I worked at a bank first for four years."*

*Because he knew people on the floor, and because his wife was in full agreement that he should give it a shot, John began clerking at the Board of Trade in 1988. Within two months, fate moved him to the next level. A friend planned to take a two-month vacation, so John offered to lease his seat during his absence.*

*That led to a two-year apprenticeship in which John traded outright positions in the municipal bond pit. The market tended to not support that kind of activity—most of the successful muni traders were spreading other markets against it. John couldn't do that because his small seat provided only limited market access. Although he wasn't actually losing money during the time, he was finding his initiation frustrating.*

*"I almost quit a few times," he admitted. "My wife kept me in it, thank God."*

*Again, it's a recurrent theme of this book that a trader's success closely mirrors the support he receives outside the market arena. John described his wife, Beth, as "a strong woman—stronger than me." She had no trading background herself—just a belief in her husband's potential.*

*John also befriended several "emotionally supportive" people in the pit "who I believed in, and they believed in me."*

*John is likeable and easygoing enough to where that's not surprising. The customary pit aggression might seem less characteristic of him, although I remember witnessing a few of his intense exchanges during my abbreviated pit career. (Not that his success wouldn't provide sufficient proof-in-the-pudding).*

*At any rate, John was emotionally fortified enough to survive his learning curve. "For any newcomer in any field, you need at least two years to give it a shot," he observed in retrospect.*

*His quantum leap occurred when he started leasing the larger associate membership seat, which allowed him to flash orders into adjoining interest rate pits. His resulting new career as an intermarket spreader took off almost immediately.*

*"I put on munis against 30-year bonds... against 10-year notes. I liked the relative safety."*

*He gradually eased into each new career phase—not forcing too much too soon.*

*"A big mistake traders make is trying to start out too quickly," he said. "They buy or lease more than they initially need. Unless you get into a big overhead situation right away, your initial investment is not that great."*

*For over a decade, he remained in the same pit. Then when volume dropped precipitously by the late 90s, like several other fellow muni locals, John found his way to the Board's new ten-year agency pit in spring, 2000. Now he's putting on spreads with exotic new aconyms, such as the "FYT" (five year over ten year notes) and the TAG (ten year over agencies). Typically, he had little trouble getting re-acclimated, and in these days of rampant pessimism over anything floor-related, he actually sees potential in the contract.*

*His trading style encompasses some technical analysis and a lot of intuition. Typically, he views weekly charts first, and narrows his focus down to 60-minute bars. He studies outright and spread charts, comparing two or three markets to determine overall direction as well as relative strength among them. He also utilizes moving average crossovers, and is a big advocate of "follow the trend."*

*By 1991, he was routinely trading 20 to 25 lots and building up to positions of 100 spreads or more. There was nothing unusual about the 150 spreads he came in with on the day the bottom fell out of the muni-30-year bond spread.*

---

It was fall, 1994, and John McCracken was one of several people in the muni pit that was getting long the MOB spread (long munis, short bonds) as the close approached.

"They got us slowly suckered in," John remembered. "They made it look a little too attractive."

Orange County, California was one day away from publicly announcing that it was defaulting on its municipal bonds. A common hard-to-dispute trader belief is that a select few group of market players inevitably have advance information about announcements, reports, etc. The munis kept being offered lower and lower at seemingly attractive levels. John McCracken's job was to buy what appeared undervalued. He continued to do so, all the while spreading off his longs by shorting 30-year bonds.

The position came back slightly by the close, so John felt OK about his large holdings. The next morning, however, the spread opened roughly 10 ticks in the wrong direction and grew steadily worse.

John immediately sensed that something was wrong. All the action was muni-related; had the bonds followed appreciably lower, his losses would have been mitigated. Unfortunately, the bonds were hardly budging during the muni rout.

Implementing his usual methodology, John initially faded the move. As the munis were offered ever lower, John bought more and continued to offset them in the bonds. He was adding to his position; a common practice among professionals, albeit one discouraged in the public sector.

"Cannonballing is usually a good strategy, but we like to call it 'price averaging'," said John. "The trick is to do it only one time; you're in the position, it's hurting you, and you look for one more spot. Maybe you wait for the panic to stop, and you try to add then. If that fails, then you say 'forget it.' The biggest mistake a trader makes is trying to defend a position."

In the approximate hour between the opening and the time the news actually hit, John had already thrown in the towel. The pre-news market melt had him down around $120,000.

Without missing a beat, he reflexively began reversing his muni position to the short side and by the end of the day, had recovered $30,000. Three days later, with the market still roiling over the news, John had recouped his entire loss.

"It was the best trading week of my life," said John. "I broke even. It was like, you know what? I know I can handle trading now!"

As for his evolving emotional state throughout the incident, John claimed, "It didn't really bother me, surprisingly. It was just one of those things you knew could happen.

"At the end of that first day, I went home and told my wife, 'aah, I lost a little money, don't worry about it'."

John shrugged and took a sip of water. "You're not going to last if you let it phase you. When it starts to affect you, you have to leave."

# Steve Moore

## Chapter 30

# Steve Moore

## "They're Ringing Bells, Something's Wrong."

*Steve Moore is president of Moore Research Center, Inc., (MRCI). The company furnishes historical charts, graphs and other computer data to a subscriber base that includes several major brokerage houses. It has been featured in The Wall Street Journal and Investor's Business Daily, and is a part of Linda Bradford Raschke's website, which MRCI set up. The Chicago Mercantile Exchange and Board of Trade have also utilized the service for some of their historical year-end publications. The company offers mainly seasonally related weekly and monthly commentary by Steve and other staff members over its website, www.mrci.com.*

*Steve was active in computer programming since the pre-PC mid -seventies, (back when computers were run by little Flintstone birds on treadmills). He honed his abilities from scratch off university-owned systems starting with sophisticated regression analysis models. He instinctively knew it would all somehow tie into other pursuits, including investing, which he'd also begun exploring in the seventies.*

*His father was a partner in a wood products firm, for which Steve set up a futures trading division in 1977. He started trading related commodities—lumber and plywood—but eventually branched off into all markets. His signals were a combination of computer-generated momentum and overbought-oversold indicators.*

*As a result of his computer and advisory services as well as his personal trading success, Steve lives the good life on a scenic 73-acre ranch just outside of Eugene, Oregon. The complex houses his office and residence, as well as a grass tennis court and three hole golf course.*

---

As with so many of the profiles depicted within these pages, Steve Moore's most significant setback occurred on tail end of a big market success. He was trading three accounts, one personal, one with his father, and one with his father and a handful of other partners. In short, Steve had the biggest overall interest; a lot at stake when, in late 1981, he was short a number of heating oil contracts.

"It wasn't a hedge," said Steve. "I was doing a lot of spec trades at the time."

The market broke hard, and Steve booked his first six-figure winner.

"We were young and didn't know much about futures, but boy, it was really easy to make a lot of money!"

Actually, even that trade hadn't exactly been a free ride. Before it finally paid off, it had moved up to pressure-point-levels, causing Steve some memorable sleepless nights.

"You know the feeling of waking up and you're soaked in sweat. There was some pain before we made all that money."

But once the happy ending arrived, Steve was succumbing to the classic "nothing-can-touch-me-now" mindset. He immediately began searching for another world to conquer.

In the two months of his oil success, another wild ride had been occurring in the live cattle market. According to Steve, the February 1982 contract went from a November $66 high to $53 a month later, and then it rallied, broke and rallied yet again into early January. His computer was alerting him of a "greatly overbought" situation. He began selling cattle, and shortly after, initiated shorts in pork bellies and live hogs as well.

The meats trade at their limit positions far more frequently than any other futures complex. This fact made the findings of Steve's acquaintance, Bob Howe, director of research at Lincoln-Staley, especially relevant.

Howe felt that daily limit moves were an especially reliable indicator of future price action. MRCI tested his theories and came up with "Howe's Limit Rule." It in essence says that when a market hits limit up or down, the odds are great that it will return to that level and take it out, probably within one day, and almost certainly within a few.** This raises interesting implications. A short term trader might confidently buy a pullback off limit-up, for example. He or she might reasonably hold an existing position into limit knowing that better exit opportunities will almost certainly follow.

---

** A belly system of mine, disclosed in my first book, *Market Rap: the Odyssey of a Still Struggling Commodity Trader*, capitalized on this very phenomenon. Basically, the system would get long as the market approached limit up, and short near limit down. It would attempt to get out the next day at that limit—the obvious hope being that the opening would gap and provide an even better exit—maybe at yet another limit. The system consistently made money for years, and I only recently retired it due to a precipitous drop in volume.

Steve affirmed that other traders were profiting in pretty much the same way, although he asked me not to point that out. "Why not?" I asked. "Because," he replied, " people would start trying to do it, and it's the most nerve wracking thing in the world." "Well, I'll put it in, but I'll include your disclaimer that it would be nerve wracking and hard for almost anybody to do," I said. You stand warned.

---

One thing a believer in Howe definitely would not want to do, of course, is be short against limit up, but unfortunately,

Steve wasn't aware of the stat at the time. All he knew was that his computer was generating short signals, he believed in his methodology and besides; he had just made a bundle.

The second thing Steve didn't know at the time was how strong the seasonal January uptrend is in meats. Even though he believed in the vastly overbought condition indicated by his model, even though he suspected the upward movement was ultimately going to be proven false, he couldn't continue to fight it. He was overexposed for one thing, having routinely added ten lots with each new trade to all three markets. In a classic case of emotional trading, he kept increasing his size as the market lurched ever higher. He described himself as being "short a bundle" when the first limit-up move hit.

Through scrambling senses, Steve watched the next day as it rallied a little beyond that point. He sold some more. He endured another limit or two, and then added still more shorts the first day the markets opened lower. Naturally, that didn't represent the turning point—merely a pause before the relentless advance continued.

"As they take it and go back the other way, the market is now trading you, you're not trading it," Steve observed. "Now you're just trying to do damage control.

"Finally, I reached a point where I knew it was just ludicrous," he said. "I had lost nearly my entire oil profit. It was a humiliating experience. What it does to you mentally is, you don't feel like getting up in the morning."

It took him about a year to reclaim his equilibrium. He described his learning curve as "tough and expensive," but as is frequently recounted, ultimately a catalyst for better trading. Steve went back to the drawing board and greatly improved his computer model. Part of the revamping was to incorporate seasonal considerations, as well as Howe's Limit Rule, into his methodology.

And, of course, he seriously reflected on what had gone wrong.

"I had just made a whole bunch of money and so then I increased my trading size," he concluded. "I probably bet way too big a percentage, because when you've got that many contracts on, and they start moving limit against you, it doesn't take many days like that to wipe you out.

"I took a bad position and made it worse. I kept figuring that the market was wrong, just overreacting to short-term weather.

"I didn't recognize the urgency of limits. It taught me that the first limit against you, *get out.* It's telling you that there's an imbalance—they're ringing bells, something's wrong."

As a trader is sinking into the whirlpool, thoughts of better times seem far removed, intangible. It's hard to imagine what it will feel like to get past the nightmare; to see the light at the end of the tunnel, to merely be able to breathe again. During the ordeal, Steve made a pact with his wife. If this thing ever turns around, he said, if we can ever get out of this hole, let's take the kids to Disneyland.

About a year later, after Steve's new foundation was in place and his trading was once again a profitable venture rather than a leaky sieve, they did just that. Miles from home, Steve was experiencing something he could barely imagine a year earlier; an $8,500 profit in a fresh trade. As he'd fantasized throughout his ordeal, the occasion was one he could savor beyond almost anything else within memory—better than the previous windfalls that dwarfed it.

It's all in the perception. As Steve put it, "We had the best vacation of our lives."

*Bob Martin*

## CHAPTER 31

# BOB MARTIN

## "I WANTED TO GET MY MONEY BACK IN PRETTY MUCH THE WAY I'D LOST IT—RAPIDLY."

*Bob Martin was launching his trading career at the same time I began stealing days off from my then-existing position as car agency manager. I too was the owner of a Mid America commodity seat, and any morning I could get free, I'd make my hour-and-a- half pilgrimage to the floor. Bob was a part of a small assemblage of grain traders representing the other side of a wall I longed to break through. Not since high school had I envied a clique more.*

*Back in 1982, his neophyte status had escaped me. He was scalping corn and wheat with apparent ease and confidence, and by the end of his first trading year, had run his initial $2,500 trading stake up to $30,000—at the time, not bad for a kid just out of college.*

*Perhaps it was in his blood. His grandfather was Mayor Daly's bodyguard—one of several police officers who would discover that the Board of Trade was a prudent place to venture during their unconventional off-hours.*

*Bob's grandfather subsequently enjoyed a successful 40-year run at the Board, and his father, uncle, and other relatives also acquired memberships. The family offered assistance in buying his seat, but Bob's skinny account startup was his own.*

*"My dad felt that commodities was something you really had to want," said Bob, "and the easiest way to find out if you wanted it or not was to use your own money."*

*Bob came to agree with his father's assessment that substantial startup endowments have tended to create recklessness and complacency within novices. "I've seen it happen enough times—when they're given a lot, boom, they just go through it."*

*He continued to perform respectably in the corn and wheat futures pits. Then in 1985, the Midam introduced options on futures. The wheat option contract became one of their nearly unprecedented primary markets—neither the Board of Trade nor anyone else offered it.*

*He and his circle of friends pounced on the opportunity to become market makers. Bob began holding huge, complicated positions. Soon after, he found himself facing his first destabilizing loss.*

*His holdings were downside-friendly as the Chernobyl disaster story broke. Wheat had been called limit down, and Bob was anticipating a windfall. Two minutes before the opening, the initial reports hit and the market opened limit up. His unrealized mega-gain had become a problem that was threatening to become catastrophic.*

*He survived, although not without scars. ("Not only had I lost money, but now I had a lingering psychological fear of what could happen"). Nevertheless, he kept his eye on the ball, and the wheat option pit resumed serving as his steadfast gateway to the next level.*

*Bob and his fellow market makers were in position to migrate to the CBOT just as the Board was threatening to obliterate the Midam's contract with a wheat option pit of its own. The timing was significant for another reason; it occurred shortly before the drought of 1988. Bob was able to build a significant economic base from that, despite suffering his near-Waterloo within the period. His success moved him from the options to the wheat futures pit in 1988, and in 1991, to the Chicago Stock Exchange.*

*He currently is a market maker for 22 different stocks. His technique hasn't changed since his post-Mega Loss futures trading days. In contrast to the era before, in which he'd continually live with a giant latticework of positions, he is usually able to get flat now thanks to the electronic market.*

*"It makes for less stress." Bob's definition of stress: "The inability to attain unrealistic expectations."*

---

Bob Martin estimated that during the Board of Trade's 1987 wheat option pit inception, "maybe 40 to 50 traders and five or six brokers" were standing in the pit. Eight months later, he was one of roughly six locals and three brokers who remained. His significantly increased pie portion resulted in his best year to date.

"Then 1988 arrived," said Bob, "and volume started going up and up and up. When the drought hit, it just got beyond belief. Fantastic...beyond my wildest dreams.

"At the time, I probably had limit positions across the board in wheat options, and pretty close to it in corn. Plus, large positions in the soybean options as well. Everything was working out well."

He was engaged to be married, and decided he could easily afford a new house. Again, things were great, but again, we're talking futures markets where fortunes can change on a dime.

"Sometimes you have a tendency to confuse that first really good market with being a good trader," said Bob. "I was thinking that my years of hard work were finally paying off and that I was getting to the point where I was a successful trader. Furthermore, I was going to be a successful trader from then on."

Hardly unreasonable, considering that his relatives had for decades enjoyed such a life.

With three weeks to go before expiration, he was in a limit September position, and long premium across the board. (Call options increase in value as the market moves higher, puts do the same as it drops. Being long everything, his best-case scenario was that the market would continue to trend dramatically in either direction, and his worst nightmare was that it wouldn't move at all. In the latter case, everything he bought would dramatically lose value or expire worthless).

When your position sheets start to resemble a phone book, however, other things can go wrong as well. Bob was discovering that he couldn't trust his option-pricing model.

"My system showed that the most I could lose at the time was $200,000, which was a risk I was willing to assume. But after the first week, I lost $250,000, and my position still showed me with the capability of losing another $200,000. That got me a little concerned."

On Friday with two weeks left before expiration, the market opened limit up, and from there, began a steady decline. In an ideal world, Bob could have cashed in a significant amount of his exploding calls, but his very size in the market was precluding that. (By his estimation, he was accounting for about 80 percent of the pit's activity). There wouldn't be nearly enough interested buyers.

He therefore did what size traders normally do in that situation; he sold futures against his position. Unfortunately, due to exchange limits, he couldn't sell enough to significantly alleviate the risk he'd been building.

"I was able to sell about a million and a half (bushels of) wheat, pretty close to the limit."

He'd needed more like four million. He made $500,000 that day, a lot of money by anybody's standards, but he was painfully aware of how vulnerable he was becoming. He had not done enough to shield himself from the possibility of an inert market developing at the worst possible time.

The following Monday, he again studied his pricing system, and concluded that he was at risk for $400,000—again an acceptable worst-case scenario considering what he'd just earned. With ten days left in the options, Bob entered a nightmare.

"The market didn't trade for two weeks," he recounted. "It stayed within a seven or eight cent range."

The market had found a home close to the strikes where Bob had his biggest positions. If you're long, the price increases the further into your direction it goes. In Bob's case, a distance in either direction would have helped.

The model was again inaccurate; on the final option attrition, Bob dropped more than double its worst-case projected $400,000. Factoring in his gain of two weeks earlier, his net loss came to about $400,000. He still was having an overall good year, but obviously, few could survive such an experience emotionally unscathed.

"It was stunning to say the least. It really affected my confidence. Not only did I have the big loss, but then the markets changed. We lost the commercial-based trade, and it was difficult to make any money."

Bob then started thinking along the lines of anxious high rolling gamblers.

"I don't know if this is typical human response, but I wanted to get my money back in pretty much the manner in which I'd lost it—rapidly."

The attitude merely prolonged Bob's ineffectiveness for another couple of months.

"I started trading larger and larger, trying to get my money back," said Bob, "and I was unable to. I probably lost a little more during that period.

"My confidence was shaken, and fear came into play again, because I'd still had a very large position going into 1989—the March and July expirations. I became suspect of my option pricing system, and was fearful that if it was wrong as much as it was in the September options, then my potential loss in the upcoming months could be quite a bit higher."

It's not easy to throw out something within which there is such a huge personal investment, but Bob knew he had no choice. He went into a defensive mode, hedging his existing position as best he could. He lost a little more, but became reconciled to the expediency of lessening his exposure.

"Then, I took three weeks off. I'd never really taken more than a day or two off before, I love that place so much, but I had to get my head back together."

He identified overtrading and greed as the twin catalysts behind his reversal. The latter had reached its apex during wheat's limit up opening. Bob had been anticipating returns in the "make-your-whole-career-and-retire" strata. He would have gotten it had the market stayed locked limit up through just one additional session.

He concluded that the true foundation for his success had been smaller, steadier profits that relied less on long-ball hitting. He began using a method his grandfather had touted for years. He started trading for eighth cent ticks. He aimed for $1,000 per day profits.

Once he lost the idea of chasing his losses, he was back in his groove. He had made a major trading adjustment—no longer would previous activity color what he had to do at present in the market. He'd try to learn from his losses, but beyond that, he'd write them off and move on.

Today he enjoys far more of that frequently touted "balance" in his life. There are no more nights when he walks up and down the Gold Coast into the wee hours as he had done in his most frenzied days. He follows trends longer, so that smaller sizes carry more punch. He trades with more consistency and less risk. He can do so and still enjoy what for him is unprecedented financial returns. (As of this January 2001 writing, 2000 was his most successful trading year).

"I can still make the '88 money today," said Bob, "only now, there won't be the same death blow if it doesn't go.

"It's a much more enjoyable, peaceful way of life."

*Bill Kragie*

have some good trading opportunities here." While he admittedly didn't know the full extent of Bill's open losses, he did agree with Bill that they were witnessing an aberrant situation.

By noon, the worst was over. The next day, Bill had to meet a margin call, but neither that nor anything else did much to alter his long term approach, his original intent. In the ensuing days and weeks, he was able to recoup all his losses, and finished his year at a higher equity level than at the onset of the drawdown.

"It was either going to work and I was going to make money, or I was going to walk out of here with a $100,000 debit," Bill said flatly.

Bill obviously spends a lot less time fretting over unpleasant "what-ifs" than do a lot of traders. In times of extreme stress, does he ever contemplate the possibility of having to give up his trading life, of having to start over in another field? What would that portend for him?

"If you've been somewhat successful in the business, and honest, with what it's trained you to do, you should be able to walk into any other business and there should be symmetry—similar application.

"To be able to think logically, quickly on your feet in special situations...show me a situation you couldn't apply it to."

But despite the apparent overall soundness of his strategy...wasn't he crossing good money management boundaries? In retrospect, was his risk reasonable?

"The investor can stay home and buy and never sell short. We as traders serve an economic function—we accommodate them and short the market.

"You know," you can almost hear him shrug through the phone line, "we're traders. We're supposed to take heat. That's why we're on the floor."

~

*Tom Murray*

## CHAPTER 33

# TOM MURRAY

## "I'LL MUSCLE THE MARKET WHEN I SHOULD HAVE JUST GOTTEN OUT AND GONE ON TO A BETTER TRADE."

*Tom Murray is widely acknowledged to be one of the biggest presences in the Chicago Board of Trade corn pit. His ascent was swift and steady; from the time he began brokering in 1988 and independently trading shortly thereafter through the present, he has more or less consistently increased his prominence on a yearly basis.*

*We were introduced for the first time during lunch, and I quickly surmised that the image I was getting across the table was different from that of his pit persona. Despite his large physical stature and reputation for occasional heated exchanges, Tom was low keyed and reticent. His observations were succinct and informative, but for more expansive answers, he sometimes had to be prodded.*

*He kind of epitomized the "gentle giant." His voice was a raspy near-whisper, although he attributed that to a cold rather than any pit-related histrionics.*

*"I have a good pit voice," he assured me. "People know where I stand. I yell a lot."*

*Allowing himself to be baited into personal altercations, in fact, is what Tom sees as his greatest weakness. He's never been fined for fight-related infractions, but as he put it, "I argue a lot. I let personalities get to me."*

*He added, "Sometimes you get mad because you missed the market, and it's a form of not being disciplined. It should have been yours, you yell at someone, you try to protect your position, so you sell another three or four hundred...."*

*"You try to muscle the market?" I asked.*

*"Yeah, that's my biggest problem. I'll muscle the market when I should have just gotten out and gone onto a better trade. I let myself get irritated and wind up doing something I wouldn't normally want to do."*

*Aside from that, Tom regards himself as being well suited to the pit trading dynamic. He's large, loud, and not shy about protecting his turf. He trades size, he's a reliable, straight-shooting presence, and so brokers routinely rely on him. He regards aggressiveness as a key to market success; in his opinion, people with athletic backgrounds have an edge. (He was active in all major sports in high school).*

*Tom hails from a family of thirteen children. He was the second of his siblings to venture onto the floor, and the first to undertake life as an independent trader. (Today, out of five brothers and one brother-in-law in the business, three trade for themselves full time).*

*Tom's normally supportive wife, Jackie, was nervous about his big step. True, the Murray family had three generations of market history behind them, but it had always been in the brokerage arena where consistent income is a certainty. Tom's recently retired father, for example, had held a large deck for over forty years. He was in favor of his son's move, however, having witnessed Tom's swift assimilation of trading techniques. He helped his son purchase the seat.*

*"He thought I was talented," said Tom. "He saw me move quick, he thought I was good at it. He would have made the same move himself except he had thirteen kids to support; he didn't feel he could make the transition and give up the deck."*

*Tom was able to allay his wife's anxiety in short order—the usual learning curve tuition lasted "maybe two or three months." By his second year, he had already arrived—a full time independent trader earning a decent living. With each successive year, he steadily increased his income by an estimated 20-40 percent.*

*His progression mirrored his increasing reliance on the mechanics of the pit as opposed to arbitrary initiation of positions. In an era when most traders are complaining that the floor edge is vanishing, Tom considers himself to be pretty much a pure scalper. He'll sometimes venture into other grain pits to put on an intermarket spread, but within his home court, his activity is pretty much confined to supplying a steady stream of bids and offers. (This is not to say he always insists on the edge. He couldn't be such a prominent force were that the case).*

*"I became a lot more disciplined," said Tom. "I'd 'hand in cards' (scalp) rather than trade positions, and the more I did that, the more the money came my way."*

*In 1996, during record low supply stocks and a weather scare, corn began a dizzying ascension to over five dollars a bushel. In that time of nearly unprecedented volatility, Tom enjoyed his first financial quantum leap. As has been recounted many times, however, such prosperity often serves as a prelude to a big fall. In Tom's case, the bottom dropped out during one wild day.*

---

I've noticed over the years that scalpers, despite their relatively high success rates, tend to be the least historically attuned traders. Sometimes they've been unable to recall a previous day's high or low for example. It's just not always relevant to their ability to make money.

When one does something well enough that it's second nature, stepping back and dissecting it, let alone imparting it to others, can be difficult. Tom Murray best recalls general things about his trading history; how he went from handling a sell stop order deck in the corn pit to adding personal trading to his activity, and then jettisoning the brokerage entirely. He remembers improving as his trading horizon shifted from longer positions to shorter sprint-like scalps. As a natural outflow of that, he would take bigger orders from the brokers, and as his commitment got bigger still, they were suddenly seeking him out. It became a thing that fed on itself.

During the wild corn market of 1996, Tom was immersed in his activity, cranking out trades in machine-like fashion. What he considered to be average good and bad days alike involved about $10,000 to $15,000. Win or lose, he was one of the pit's main market makers. (Bruce Williams described him as *the* biggest corn trader. Tom acknowledged that as far as scalpers go, that could be close to the truth, but some of the spreaders routinely traded larger).

On the other hand, Tom remembers nothing particularly extraordinary about the event he describes as "my first crushing blow— the day I got my ass kicked." It occurred in the middle of the month. It was volatile, but so were most days at the time. He can't provide an exact historical context although the mechanics of what went wrong remain all too clear in his memory.

"I kept getting long and long and more long," he said. "Then I puked at the bottom and I got flipped around and got very short at the worst level. Then they came for the stuff and rallied it about five cents in my face."

He was doing what he normally did—fielding orders. Unfortunately, sometimes the market is less merciful than others as far as how it lets you resolve your positions.

Tom lost $150,000—about ten to fifteen times his normal "bad day." Despite a prior account runup, he suddenly found himself in a cash crunch. He had to borrow $50,000 from his father, and make special arrangements with his clearing house.

It was volatility that perhaps made him a little too loose prior to the hit and volatility that both tagged him and then ultimately bailed him out. (Yet another recurring theme). He had been steadily increasing his size, as the market got more volatile—something he now regards as ill advised. Rather than chase his losses, Tom abruptly shifted gears.

"Most good traders, when they go bad like that, just go back to the basics—to what made them successful in the first place. I started trading smaller and more disciplined."

In the last two weeks of the month, he averaged plus $10,000 a day. By the end of it, he was even. He paid his father back.

What had gone wrong? Tom identified a dual problem—over-leverage combined with a relatively unfamiliar trading style.

"I was just taking everything the brokers were offering," he said. "I was trading about four or five times my normal unit size. I was cannonballing."

"Naturally, everybody says you should stick to what you're good at—try to make your ten to fifteen thousand a day, right? Well, sometimes you get a little greedy—with a good market, you tend to think there's more that can be taken out.

"Whenever you're trading a style you're not accustomed to, and the numbers are bigger than you're used to trading, you trade differently, you make mistakes. It becomes hard to make rational decisions. It causes you to do dumb stuff that you normally wouldn't do."

Today, despite an even greater stature, Tom isn't timid about accommodating only part of an order, or just flat out telling brokers he doesn't want any more. He'll normally hold overnight positions, but won't do so if big gap openings are probable, such as during weather markets. He feels no pressure to do anything more than earn money in the ways that are most comfortable for him.

He's a self-described optimist—a fact that became apparent in various ways. He had an interesting response when I asked him how his wife felt about his loss. She was worried, he admitted, but supportive. Did he find outside support from friends and loved ones to be crucial to trading success as had been recounted by so many others? Yes, he said, if his wife hadn't been supportive, it would have taken him longer to earn back his money.

Note that he didn't say, "I wouldn't have been able to earn back the money." The idea of outright failure just isn't on his radar screen.

He is also upbeat about his personal future. He echoed other traders who feel that the agricultural markets aren't as readily vulnerable to impending online conversion as are the financials. There doesn't seem to be the kind of race to implement screen trading on either a replacement or simultaneous trading basis. Tom expects to be doing his current thing for at least another fifteen years.

"If I'm forced to trade online, I'll lose a lot of the elements that make me successful," he observed. "But I'll gain in other respects. With my style of trading, I'll step out a lot of times. On the screen, if they're offering nines and I'm willing to buy them, I know that I'll get them. I won't have to worry about a broker falling asleep or merely hitting the guy next to him."

Not even a potential revamping of his comfortable environment would throw him. He's not at the alarmist extreme of the "future of trading" projections, but even if the doomsayers prove correct, Tom will adapt.

"I'm always positive," he summarized. "My glass is always half full.

"Ninety percent of the business is confidence. Once you lose that, you might as well get out of the pit."

~

*Ruth Barrons Roosevelt*

# Chapter 34

## Ruth Barrons Roosevelt

## "The Wildness Lies in Wait."

*Ruth Barrons Roosevelt perfectly articulated what must be a universal feeling in the trading world.*

*"I remember the first time I was looking at a Reuter's screen," she said. "I said, 'all I have to do is be right.' It maybe sounds silly, but I was so into the idea that you don't have to please other people. You don't have to overcome any prejudices. All you have to do is be right. It's between you and the markets."*

*Finding the correct path, of course, is easier said than done; the subject of innumerable books, essays, and private odysseys. Any insider will tell you that it's a long and winding road to trading competence, let alone greatness. That first beckoning idea, however, that market success is theoretically 100 percent attainable by solitary effort, is such an awesome lure. Once it becomes your driving force, re-routing into other mindsets becomes all but impossible.*

*Ruth began trading her own futures account in 1979, some time after earning her law degree. She quickly moved into brokerage and money management. Her former employers include Drexel Burnham Lambert, and Thomson McKinnon Securities Inc., of which she was a Vice President. She headed the International Moneyline Trading Desk at Rudolf Wolf, New York, from 1981 through 1986.*

*Today, Ruth trades individual stocks and mutual funds and occasionally futures for herself. Perhaps her greater fame, however, stems from her involvement in today's flourishing trader psychology industry.*

*"In 1992, I stopped being a broker and became a trading coach," said Ruth. "I work with traders all over the world to help them handle psychological aspects of trading."*

*Her methodology includes Neuro-Linguistic-Programming, behavior modification and hypnosis. The core idea behind the treatment is that thought patterns influence trading results. Some deeply imbedded beliefs are sure-fire catalysts for failure. Through an interactive analysis accommodating the trader's specific situation, Ruth has purportedly turned many chronic losers into consistent money-makers, as well as improved the performance of the already highly successful.*

*It's not an overnight miracle cure. The process takes a minimum of three months. "Change is incremental," Ruth explained.*

*She begins by having the trader provide an "outcome statement;" a list of intended objectives. Once the desire is made clear-cut and non-conflicted, Ruth's task is to route her client's behavior as quickly and directly as possible toward the goal.*

*"We look at what's working. I help them do more of that. We look at what is not working. I help them stop that. We test out what might work. We look at what beliefs are getting in the way of their trading and we replace them with more affirming beliefs. We look at what associations they're making."*

*After each session, Ruth makes a self-hypnosis tape addressing the trader's personal issues. The trader listens during the week and continues to do phone exercises with her. Since most of Ruth's clients are outside of her New York area, most of the coaching is done over the phone.*

*"I work with traders who are the best in the world...and some of the worst. Plus a lot of in-between.*

*"I assist traders who are holding on by their fingernails, and others who have millions and millions under management and are very good traders. They work with me for insurance, to make sure they're continuing to go with their strengths."*

*Ruth asserts that practically every client has provided her with insight, which she has re-incorporated into both her teaching and writings. She has contributed numerous articles on trading psychology to "Stocks and Commodities" magazine. She wrote the acclaimed book,* ***Exceptional Trading: The Mind Game.*** *(Among the notables offering testimonials; trading psychologist Van Tharp and fellow NLP specialist Adrienne Laris Toghraie). She also co-authored* ***Living In Step*** *with Jeanette Lofas, and has just written* ***Twelve Habitudes of Highly Successful Traders,*** *published by Traders Press, Inc.*

*Her reputation has led to appearances on The Today Show, Good Morning America, and Late Night With David Letterman. Her work has been profiled in "Business Week," "Barron's," (no relation), and "The New York Times."*

*"My work is geared strictly toward getting results," said Ruth. "Whatever works— NLP, hypnosis. We don't dig around looking for something terrible and study why you're doing it. That's not what I'm about. I'm about making change in the quickest way possible."*

*Ruth has a way of distilling familiar yet not easily defined ideas and experiences into succinct adages. They alone might warrant her inclusion in this book. Ruth however, has done more than study the phenomenon of trading from the outside looking in—she herself has been in the belly of the beast. What follows is her own unique dance on the ledge, (plus some added insights).*

---

"Successful traders have an attitude or consciousness of 'abundance'," said Ruth Barrons Roosevelt. "They don't come from 'lack.' If you come from 'lack' or 'scarcity,' you're going to make a thousand different errors."

Ruth was expressing a variation on the well-known trader maxim "don't trade with scared money." Somehow, though, her take brought new light to the old concept. It's not just about being scared and under-funded. There's an implied flip side also—winning traders are detached, aloof. They may even be bored with their trading because their overall outcome is so predictable yet un-dramatic. Since they control their risk so well, they've diminished the possibility of heart-pounding exciting surprises.

Sometimes, mechanical system traders will lament that their methodology is consistently profitable, but dull. Ruth has suggested that they continue to commit the bulk of their money to their proven approaches, but that they should also open a small account for the purpose of "playing" with some money. It often behooves even the most routine system grinders to let off steam once in a while.

"The word 'gamble' is actually derived from 'gambol', which means 'to play'," Ruth observed. "Play is fine. Gambling is alright as long as you're not habitually losing."

Perhaps her own advice would have saved her from her most destabilizing loss. It unfortunately occurred early in her career, before she had accumulated so much wisdom from so many traders. She had a consistent moneymaking idea she started taking for granted and unfortunately, no small account to act as a release valve.

"I was trading gold," said Ruth. "It was the early eighties, a time when the market was moving very fast."

It was also the days before computerized charts, and traders busied themselves with a variety of left field ideas that seemed to work—for a while.

"I don't recommend this," said Ruth, "but I would develop a view as to whether the trend was up or down. Then I'd buy or sell ten contracts at tops and bottoms of ranges. My purpose was to get a dollar ($1000)—all I needed."

Ruth reasoned that since she was entering at support and resistance levels, if the market moved three dollars against her, a probable breakout was commencing that would figure to go further. She would then reverse at the three-dollar point so that she was again net long or short ten contracts. She'd play the second trade for greater magnitude—hoping to at least recover the earlier three-point loss, and possibly net a profit besides.

"I was making a thousand a day," said Ruth. "It seemed easy."

So easy that Ruth decided she could squeeze two trades a day out of it and earn herself $2,000. For a time, even that worked.

It was an idea guaranteed to have a high percentage of wins verses losses. The problem, of course, would be what would happen on the days where you couldn't ring the cash resister at either of the two levels.

On a day during the Falkland Islands crisis, Ruth obtained her expected $1,000 on her first trade. Then she entered Trade 2 on the long side. As always, she had her contingency reverse stop up—sell 20 contracts to get her short.

It was to become a classic case of "the best laid plans...." Out of nowhere, the market broke $35, and Ruth flashed on the idea that her stop was filled way above where the market was now languishing, and that she was about to book a huge net winner.

She wasn't taking into consideration the possibility of horrendous fills. Prices don't always move in an incremental tick-by-tick fashion—they sometimes gap immediately to a new level. (For further reference, check out the surprise federal interest rate cuts beginning in 1998, or numerous other general instances where sudden shocking news blindsides a market).

As Ruth later learned, she wasn't executed three dollars down, nor anywhere near it. She was filled at the very bottom, as if there had been no intermediate trades at all. (Sometimes there literally aren't).

Her ten longs, offset $35 lower, cost her $35,000. She was also *short* ten contracts at that level. The price then slingshot back in the other direction, as markets frequently do under such circumstances. She was out $10,000 on her ten shorts.

"The long and short of it was, I lost $45,000 in ninety seconds," said Ruth.

The ten shorts remained open, so Ruth had the added agony of deciding what to do with them. Not atypically, she was overwhelmed.

"I was shell shocked. At that time, $45,000 was a lot of money to me.

"I didn't know what to do, so I called one of my gurus. My voice was way high." (She amusingly re-enacted twittering hysteria). "He said, 'I told you not to overtrade!' Then he said 'get out of the position!' But I wasn't prepared to do that, so I called another friend of mine."

Her second source suggested the oft-effective idea of disengaging. Again, sometimes the trader just has to physically change something—location, activity—in order to break the paralysis.

"She told me, 'Ruth, don't sit there and watch it. Get a cup of tea. Go wash your face. I'll call around and see what I can find out.'

"I was crying. I went into the bathroom and looked at my face, all red. I'm splashing cold water on it, looking in the mirror and thinking 'is this me?'"

The friend's contact called Ruth and opined that her existing short was going to probably prove correct. He also suggested that Ruth remove half of the ten contracts so that she could more easily manage the remainder.

Ruth was grateful for the suggestion. In her volatile state, the idea hadn't even occurred to her—she'd been thinking in terms of all-or-nothing. She covered the position on five contracts. (Several days later, she would recoup the loss on the remaining five). Then she went across the street to keep an appointment she'd made with her lawyer.

"I walked right across the middle of Forty-Second Street," she said. "Nobody hit me—all the cars stopped.

"I arrived at the lawyer's office, and there were other people there. He said 'how are you?' And I held out my hands and looked at them and they weren't shaking. I said, 'I seem to be fine—I just lost $45,000 in 90 seconds'."

She had a revelation concerning the difference between people inside and outside the industry. Traders understand $45,000 lost in ninety seconds—outsiders, as a rule, can only recoil. The people overhearing the conversation appeared contemptuous...hostile.

"It was disgust and jealousy both," Ruth concluded, "that I could squander so much money. Then, I came back and there was a street vendor selling purses. I told him I wanted to buy one and he said, (condescending voice), 'it's thirty dollars!' And I said, 'so!'"

It was a variation on an oft-observed Vegas irony—we'll fret over the cost of a parking space or a steak or any number of things—and watch stoically as a stack of hundred dollar chips disappears.

"It was the oddest experience," said Ruth, "but it didn't stop me from overtrading. I did it again in the Canadian dollar."

Market lessons frequently have to be re-learned numerous times. Ultimately, Ruth received the message. To overtrade is to invite unlimited possibilities for disaster

"The wildness lies in wait," said Ruth. It's when it's the quietest that something happens."

Learning a lesson and moving on is of course it's own reward, but Ruth also got some satisfaction from how that fateful day seemingly impacted the market thereafter. Gold has been in near constant hibernation for years.

"It never traded with the same volatility. I think a lot of people got burned. The guys on the floor were ripping off people left and right. I can't say for sure, but it might have been that on that day, they killed their golden goose."

Ruth identified overtrading as her main personal mistake. She also, as a result of the event, developed better insight about losses in general. She understood that one needed to accept them, learn from them, and move on.

The people in the lawyer's office, on the other hand, suggested the kind of commonplace loss aversion that can't help but torpedo trading success. Such a phobia manifests itself in different ways. Some people can't pull the entry trigger, or they jump in late. Others hang onto ever deteriorating positions.

"A lot of people confuse loss with being wrong," said Ruth. "They feel they must be right, and that gets them into so much trouble.

"Successful people see a trade as just one point in a game. They're realistic about the present, and optimistic about the future. They think more about probabilities for success than the possibilities of what they can lose.

"They take the long term view. A loss for them is just a step on the way to a larger win. It doesn't make them a loser."

*Ray Cahnman*

# Chapter 35

## Ray Cahnman

### "You can't let liquidity force you to change the way you trade."

*Ray Cahnman is one name most frequently mentioned over the course of my interviews. In the 26 years since he started trading Ginnie Maes (mortgage backed interest futures) on the Board of Trade floor, he has impacted many lives as a fellow trader, clearing firm owner, mentor and occasional proprietary financial backer.*

*After five years as a local, Ray opened Aardvark Trading, which later became Trans marketgroup (TMG). His original motive was to be able to clear his own trades. Gradually, he added a customer base of personal associates, and people for whom they could vouch. From there, his operation expanded.*

*Of the many positions of risk in the trading world, "clearing firm owner" could well be among the most formidable.*

*"Trans marketgroup would produce statements for the traders," said Ray. "We'd handle their balances and make sure their profits or losses hit their accounts. TMG was a bookkeeper for them. For that, we got compensated with a small commission for each trade they made.*

*"Since I wasn't getting anything on their gains, I didn't want to get caught being a partner with their losses."*

*Which brings us to the main job of a clearing firm owner—to ensure that traders don't overstep their bounds to the point where the house itself becomes a co-victim. TMG managed exposure by rarely leaving a questionable stone unturned. Prospective customers were carefully screened. Active traders were consistently monitored for over-leverage or other signs of impending instability. It was essential that TMG knew what a trader's assets were, and what collateral would be available in the event of a large loss.*

*One out-of-control trader can take an entire house down in a matter of minutes. It has happened before, and Ray personally knows some of the victims. To protect TMG's interests, Ray has assumed the roles of psychologist, career counselor and friend. They have as much to gain from the interaction as he does—and vice versa.*

*"You have to know your customers," he said.*

*He is one of the more inscrutable interviewees I encountered. He was never exactly inaccessible nor abrasive, but the preliminaries of getting him to the table spanned two months. He wasn't sure how personal he wanted to be, or whether his particular version of hardship and triumph would fit in overall. He outlined general observations on losses he'd formed through years of monitoring traders. It all sounded like it would be a terrific addition to the book, but Ray wasn't sold immediately.*

*"I try to avoid publicity," he said. At one point, he threatened to pass completely, but ultimately determined that the subject matter was worth documenting.*

*One night, we had a preliminary, unofficial conversation on the subject of trader vulnerability—times to heed cautionary flags. It lasted 20 minutes, it was great, and I bemoaned the fact that I didn't have it on tape. (He kept insisting that he wasn't actually starting).*

*Once we did get rolling, I had a different challenge. Ray gave me a virtual avalanche of vital information to the point where prioritizing, categorization, etc. would prove formidable. The first night, after filling up 50 percent more tape than the standard interview, he abruptly announced, "well, I'm tired, we'll pick this up later," and then left our follow- up time ambiguous.*

*Ray has less exposure now. He recently transferred the assets of Trans marketgroup's customer operation to Fortis Bank. TMG always had two main profit centers—the floor trader clearing operation, and a branch of people hired to trade on a proprietary basis for the company account. The latter side remains operational.*

*"We could see the handwriting on the wall," Ray explained. "When trading goes all electronic, instead of serving a couple hundred customers, a clearing firm is going to have to have thousands of people in order to bring in economics of scale. TMG was in no position to do that. When the trading platform changes to all electronic, the only ones who will be in the clearing business will be large banks and institutions."*

*Throughout his career, Ray has been a "market maker." In the current electronic arena, he's one of the regular suppliers of standing bids and offers. Most traders click existing prices and are primarily racing against everyone else. The first ones in have the edge.*

*Ray is more like the guy who is setting up the playing field. Once entered, he spreads his open positions against other markets, including the cash treasuries. His edge comes from how he manages the trades once they are active.*

*Whether during normal pit hours or evening activity, there wasn't a phone conversation he didn't have to interrupt somewhere in order to trade. The years of doing it over and over obviously haven't affected his enthusiasm.*

*At one point, he said he was going to do something he didn't normally do—close out a position just so he could focus on our conversation. I held my breath—not wanting to be the cause of an unusual action resulting in a loss. I exhaled in relief once he an-*

*nounced that the move had paid off. It didn't seem like a good idea to be responsible for Ray Cahnman's losses, however inadvertently.*

---

One morning during the early nineties, Ray Cahnman watched from a just-barely safe distance as his worst nightmare played out.

"A rogue trader went nuts in the 30-year treasury bond pit," Ray recalled. "The guy didn't have any money, and he directed orders to floor brokers to sell hundreds of contracts."

He purportedly had no more than a modest five-figured equity at the time, and yet he was trading large enough to significantly move the market. By the time he was hauled out of the pit, he was millions of dollars in debt. So many other people were also affected, both positively and negatively, that it was impossible to unwind the damage.

The clearing firm sponsoring the trader was shut down the next day. It was reported that all the company's seats and assets were seized, but supposedly, even that didn't settle the debt. A high-up official purportedly had to come up with significant out-of-pocket-money besides.

The incident, as well as similar others, would be referenced many times throughout the interview. Ray Cahnman is ever cognizant of the potential devastation one renegade trader could inflict. Not even such knowledge could guarantee the safety of a clearing firm, although Ray believes that the better you know your traders, the safer you are. The victimized clearing firm might have also avoided catastrophe had more inquiries been made. Apparently, other houses had similarly had bad, albeit not fatal, experiences with the trader.

Ray's view of a good security risk pretty much dovetails with how he defines a good trader. Stable people are more likely than loose cannons to have wizard-level trading talent—skills that keep them off the brink. Just as important to trading longevity—

read stability—is an unwavering commitment to money management.

Traders have to remain liquid according to Ray. Having a lot of wealth tied into hard assets is not enough. A trader should never mentally consider a seat to be part of his or her assets. It should be a primary goal to own a home free and clear, and to avoid bank loans in general.

"Managing your liquidity extends beyond your account," said Ray. "It's about managing your life-style also. In trading, whatever you're making, you should have a life-style that reflects no more than one-half that income."

Trading is unlike any other profession due to its unpredictability. You can't "keep up with the neighbors" in the same way as other professionals with steady paychecks. All traders acknowledge the possibility of an equity drawdown, but many don't consider the full ramifications of it. Losses can lead to fear, which can lead to adverse trading adjustments.

Liquidity is the best safeguard against uncertainty—THE ultimate trader objective in Ray's mind.

"If you have a real bad day, you don't want to have to change your size because of lack of liquid capital. You may choose to do that because you don't want to get spanked two days in a row, you want to recover your rhythm or your confidence or whatever. That's OK, that's a valid choice. You just don't want to have it forced on you.

"If you decide that what happened to you was just bad luck and you then choose to trade exactly the same way, you have to have the ability to do that. You can't let liquidity force you to change the way you trade."

Ray's dreams never centered on the grandiose trader lifestyle, but on trading itself. Even after he made money, it was several years before he bought a new car. The goal was always to have the necessary ammunition—the ability to come back tomorrow.

He lost three ticks in the Ginnie Mae pit on his first trade. That amounted to $93.75 before commission, and it spooked him into standing on the sidelines for the next three days.

"It scared the hell out of me," said Ray. "I became a trader to make a living, not to lose a hundred dollars in a day!'"

He remembered his summer jobs that had paid $10 an hour. He thought of how the full contract he was leveraging on margin was actually worth $100,000. Like many other rookies, he became intimidated over the sheer magnitude of trading logistics. If you're unlucky, your fear could lead to your first destabilizing loss. Even worse, you might experience beginner's luck.

"Losing three ticks that first day made me respectful and cautious," Ray observed. "If I had made three ticks, I certainly would have traded the next day. If I'd made another three ticks or more the next day, I might have gotten cocky. Instead of one lots, I might have traded twos. I would think it was easy."

Eventually, of course, the trader's bubble will get popped. Ray's contention is that "sooner" tends to be better than "later."

"Let's say I'd been a winner pretty much on a daily basis for the first month, and that I'd accumulated quite a number of ticks. At that point, I'd be really stepping it up! If I could make money so consistently, I might as well just trade more.

"And then, you get smacked, only now, you don't just go down to zero, you go substantially through it. You're thinking you're invulnerable. When you have a loss instead of your usual winner, you think, 'hey, wait a minute. I know I'm right... I'm *always* right. The fact that the market is against me doesn't mean I'm wrong, it just means I got in a little too early. I should double up!'"

Ray's conservative temperament, combined with his early brush with reality, kept him from the extreme reversals experienced by so many others. Even a healthy respect for the market, however, won't guarantee your safety, particularly if you're forced to trade on a shoestring.

Ray's initial stake was $3,000. He had no choice but to commit a bigger percentage than what he'd subsequently risk as his account grew. Still, although he was cognizant of how tenuous his career buildup stage was, his awareness wasn't enough. To recap the theme of the interview, Ray simply lacked adequate trading liquidity. The first time it hit home was when he decided to upgrade his transportation.

"I'd always been driving total junk cars. I was saving my money. I wanted to be a trader."

Sometime around 1976, Ray figured he had enough for a new $7,000 Oldsmobile. He suffered a loss the day after he signed the papers. In Ray's mind, the price of the car was just another debit from his liquidity. Now there was an actual market loss on top of it.

Ray traded to get his deficit back—his total loss including the expenditure. Usually, that's a gateway to disaster, but Ray managed to keep his discipline in check.

"I clawed my way back," he said. "I changed my trading style. I traded a lot more cautiously."

His second near-brush with account depletion occurred just after he bought his full membership for $135,000.

"Of course when you buy it, it automatically goes down," he observed. "It dropped to around $100,000. You never buy the bottoms and sell the tops—markets are the same way."

Again, the purchase manifested itself in Ray's mind as a threat to his equity. As he fretted over another liquidity drawdown, he found himself in a large adverse calendar spread in Ginnie Mae futures.

"I was long the front months and short the back months. All of a sudden I was noticing there were no bids for spreads. I didn't know where I could get out."

Ray's reliable controlled environment had finally turned on him. He informed his clearinghouse that he might have a problem and then carried the entire position home into the weekend.

"I liquidated the following Monday. I lost all my liquidity except for the membership, and I had a sixty-five thousand dollar loan against it."

Other traders might not have regarded the situation as dire. Ray probably could have retrieved his $135,000 if he sold the seat, which would have netted him $60,000 after paying off the loan. Again, however, the hard asset didn't register on Ray's financial radar.

"It was good collateral, but I couldn't trade off it. I was reduced to trading one lots. I did so for quite a while until I was able to get enough back to trade twos and threes. I had to build it all over again right from the start.

"I got a real scare, because I could have easily blown through the seat collateral. I had a house, but my equity in that was less than $20,000. My position was such that if it would have gone a few more ticks against me, it would have taken everything and left me in a debit position."

Ray admitted he had been overtrading. Part of the problem was that the relative newness of the Ginnie market had made it hard to gage what constituted appropriate size.

Again, his reversal seemed spending-related—a stress perhaps more peculiar to Ray than the world at large. Ray, however, recognizes a universal aspect.

"Human beings in general like stability. It's particularly important for traders, because the decisions they have to make are so leveraged.

"It's not like any other profession. If a doctor or a lawyer has an off day, as all of us do, he's still going to be performing at roughly the same level. He's still going to get his paycheck. In trading, if you're a little off, the impact can be enormous.

"Even if someone makes a million dollars a year, losing days are still part of the income equation. They're going to have equity swings, and you never know where the next hit is coming from. It's stressful to buy a house and then lose six figures the next day."

Ray sees any kind of change, good or bad, as a time of necessary caution. Marriage or divorce, the death of a parent or the birth of a child alike—anything big or unusual can have an adverse performance impact.

Ray's third upheaval story centered on such a trauma. For the four years surrounding his divorce, Ray sank into a relentless professional inertia. He initially responded by cutting back on his trading. Ultimately, he decided that if successful people wanted to keep everything the same, his experiences were mandating a complete life overhaul.

"I picked up and changed environments. I moved to Australia and spent six months there. I wanted to go where nobody knew me. I took $50,000 and headed for the Sydney Futures Exchange.

"It was like I was starting completely over. Nobody knew I was a successful trader. I had to reestablish myself professionally. I had to make new friends."

His goal was to merely pay for his expenses—and snap his spell. Six months later, he would be rejuvenated enough to resume his career in Chicago, although he had done far better in Australia than merely staying afloat. It was the last time he would need a major adjustment.

Few people in the industry are as thought provoking as Ray Cahnman. (Certainly, nobody gave me nearly as much material). I heard myself laughing several times on the playback, not so much due to Ray's sense of humor, (which he has). It was more like the delight of recognition—the idea that he was articulating and validating things that so many of us have noticed for years, albeit on a more subliminal level.

Ray, for example, has his own version of "The January Effect."

"More traders have ended their careers on the first trading day in January than on any other day," said Ray. "And January as a whole has double the incidents of traders busting out as any other single month."

It comes down to a trader tendency to become bold as their trading calendar slate is again clean, and conservative once profits accrue late in the year. According to Ray, the whole process should be reversed. If you're on a roll going into the final months, you stand to gain if you can ramp up your returns. Conversely, any money you give back becomes tax-deductible, and the benefit will be felt within a few months.

People having a bad January just off a good year, on the other hand, will have a huge tax bill due in mere months, but there will suddenly be a smaller pile out of which to pay it. This is why a disproportionate number of desperate trader acts occur early in the year.

"God has a nice time hurting people in January."

Ray was warming to a subject with which most traders grapple on one subconscious level or another. Traders may live by science, but in their heart of hearts lies the uneasy suspicion that markets are more than inanimate, random movement.

"Most traders acknowledge the existence of God," said Ray. "He's up there, looking over all the people trading. And all he's doing is trying to find out that he can destroy.

"So he'll look at some rookie out there that has just stepped into something too big. He might have bought a hundred lots at ten, even though he maybe only should have been buying ten contracts.

"So God decides he can have fun with this trader. He says, 'okay, I'll make the market eleven bid—let's see if he takes his one tick profit.' God does it, and the guy buys another hundred. So God says, 'hmmm...I think I've got a live one here.'

"God knocks it down to eleven sellers and says, 'let's see if he scratches it.' He waits, and the trader doesn't do anything. So God says, 'okay, here we go,' and knocks it down a couple ticks. 'Let's see if he'll take a small loss.'

"The trader buys some more. God knows he has him now. 'Here you go,' God says, and drops it down five ticks. 'Why don't you get out? Take your loss—I know it's bigger than you wanted, but you can still save your career.'

"The guy says, 'tell you what, when it gets back to where I can average out the whole loss, I'm getting out. Please God, let it get back to that point. Let me out, and I'll never do it again.'

"Then God knows he's got him. 'Here, I'll drop it another five ticks.'"

There's probably not a trader alive who hasn't verbalized some variation of "God's out to get me— there's malice in the markets." Ray Cahnman also understands the mindset. He just doesn't have to indulge it anymore.

"God's watching me too, and maybe I make a bad trade. But God's not going to bother with me.... I won't be any fun. He knows that I have a lot of capital, and a lot of discipline."

## Recurring Kryptonite Encounters —A Summary

Many, if not most of the recounted debacles occurred on the heels of unusually profitable periods. As the trader hit a stride in which wealth accumulation seemed easy, (and like it would never stop), occasional feelings of omnipotence resulted. The descriptions of euphoria included "bulletproof," "like taking candy from a baby" and having "the walk-on-water complex."

Some would feel more relaxed about making huge purchases, or entering new positions they normally wouldn't consider. They'd try to parlay their success into markets they'd normally avoid, reasoning, "nothing can stop me." Sometimes in their casualness, they'd cancel stoplosses or haphazardly pyramid.

Others didn't succumb to such mental traps, but their particular trading styles pretty much guaranteed wide account swings. Mentally adjusting to such ups and downs is possible, but never easy, especially when the runup and giveback are so rapid-fire.

As good luck soured, the traders would respond in a few recurring ways. Those most fortunate would be able to maintain "business as usual"— trading as they always had. If an edge was meant to be taken before the crushing event, they would continue to exploit it after. Success continued to involve seizing opportunities, keeping the head down and, as Linda Raschke put it, "moving forward."

This sort of response was best exemplified by the interest rate spreaders. Most of them were too busy in the aftermath of their experiences to despair. They tended not to confuse their self-worth or abilities with isolated market events. Many verbalized variations on David Gray's "one bad thing" theme.

Those destined to prevail regarded the same volatility that had clipped them as a new source of opportunity. As a result, most made their Mega-Losses back within days.

Others were initially immobilized by their ordeals. They'd refer to themselves as being "shell-shocked," "paralyzed," or "like a zombie." It took them a beat or two to recover their professionalism; the remedy usually involved a physical change of some sort. Splashing water on the face in the bathroom. Going to the upstairs office, going for a walk—going home. Removing all or part of the position in order to "breathe easier."

If they were at their emotional limit, they'd self-impose a hiatus. It would last a day or two, or in some cases, a few months or years. Even then, however, they never totally disengaged. The off periods were used for voracious research and re-tooling of methodology. Their passions still burned unabated.

Winning traders are serious—despite loving their profession, they no longer see the point once profitability becomes impossible. This is not as simplistic as it sounds—in the world at large, there are many people trading for reasons having little to do with making money. Ego, excitement, validation...

Some of the interviewees also had to remove such imprudent driving forces from their psyches. In a game Pat Arbor described as "very psychological," large life changes were the occasional result. Joining a men's encounter group. Moving from the west to the east coast so that trading hours would be less of a drain. Re-vamping trading approaches—looking at less markets, changing horizons from short-term to long-term, or vice-versa.

And then there's the more mundane variety of day-to-day maintenance necessary for equilibrium. Routines are common with traders—an offshoot of their essential discipline. Nutrition, exercise, and yoga are frequently cited. Getting enough sleep.

Taking breaks is another biggie. It took hard work for these mavens to get where they are, but on the other hand, some trading aspects don't translate to the world at large. Work habits, for example. Some people would do well to disengage more during trading sessions. More than one person extolled the advantage of leaving, unwinding in something enjoyable like basketball, and then returning to the battlefield refreshed. Others have done well to track less markets or tune out during Globex hours. Longer and more difficult aren't always better—sometimes less *is* more.

Professionals are serious about risk management; yet seem more resistant to loss-anxiety than the public at large. Sometimes they project a near-flippancy about their huge incurred debits, which, when you think about it, is probably a crucial survival trait. To keep from getting burned, it's sometimes necessary to walk straight into the fire.

Professionals respect money, but they don't get paralyzed by it. Standard conservative financial mindsets don't always jive with trading realities. To get to your million, you might well have to face a $250,000 giveback.

So losses are inevitable—sometimes big ones. How do traders mentally navigate around them? Some advocate spending money after bad sessions. To paraphrase Larry Rosenberg, if you're only indulging yourself after hot streaks, you'll be more negatively impacted when the losses hit. Some reflexively pack up the family and hit a vacation spot. Others get their aggression out through sports.

Self-preserving philosophical adages abound: *"You can't make an omelet without breaking some eggs."*— Tony Saliba. *"I've learned to love losses."*—Charlie Wright. It seems to be a trader given that we learn more from mistakes than from triumphs.

Traders are probably more hyper-attuned and reactive to outside stimuli than most other groups. Their performances are very much impacted by events in their outside worlds.

Your best apparent chance of surviving the inevitable roller coaster ride is to have a good marriage. Over and over again, traders would cite their supportive mates as being key to why they ultimately prevailed.

Divorce represents the flip side—the number one recounted catalyst behind bad trading periods. Bruce Williams observed that an uncompassionate spouse who "doesn't understand why you have to pour your heart and soul" into your work is going be a total impediment to scaling market heights. Many others verbalized similar sentiments, or affirmed that their worst periods occurred during times of marital discord.

Poor health was the number two under miner of market success, and many traders incorporate a total well-being approach to health and fitness. Trader vocabulary is rife with such words as "focus," "timing," "rhythm," and "stamina." Exercise centers and spas are never far from exchange buildings, and local convenience stores routinely carry power snack bars.

Mental health is equally important, and depression finds a particular hot zone among traders. Some appear immune—their self-confidence and optimism acting as a shield. It would be wrong to predict that the most adept could never succumb, of course, but again, the best defense against all-encompassing despair seems to be retreat—rethink—reroute. As Damon Pavlatos observed, this is one of the few businesses where self-policing is so crucial. Part of a wizard's skill is in recognizing when to fight another day.

Balance is another trader must. Without it, you can't maintain the aforementioned attributes, such as a good marriage. Also, you risk a slippery slope if your trading priorities get screwed up. Yes, the object is to make money but no, your worth as a human does not hinge on the outcome. More than one trader learned that once the desperation for wealth vanished, the money came more easily.

And to trade, you need outside interests—a 24-7 war against the markets will kill you.

It all relates to knowing yourself. There are a multitude of approaches to market success, but all have their share of downsides. Taking a periodic, realistic self-inventory is helpful in finding the appropriate path.

Finally, when you do discover your niche, maintain continued faith in it—and yourself. Skim the last line of each of the chapters: *"I'm a fairly upbeat, optimistic person."* —Bill Beach. "Now I feel good about myself for every other reason."—Steven L. Miller.

As much as anything written, *Kryptonite* is a book about winners.

**TRADERS PRESS, INC.®**
**PO BOX 6206**
**Greenville, SC 29606**

**Publishers of:**

*A Complete Guide to Trading Profits* (Paris)
*A Professional Look at S&P Day Trading* (Trivette)
*Ask Mr. EasyLanguage* (Tennis)
*A Treasury of Wall Street Wisdom* (Editors: Schultz & Coslow)
*Beginner's Guide to Computer Assisted Trading* (Alexander)
*Channels and Cycles: A Tribute to J.M. Hurst* (Millard)
*Chart Reading for Professional Traders* (Jenkins)
*Commodity Spreads: Analysis, Selection and Trading Techniques* (Smith)
*Comparison of Twelve Technical Trading Systems* (Lukac, Brorsen, & Irwin)
*Complete Stock Market Trading and Forecasting Course* (Jenkins)
*Cyclic Analysis* (J.M. Hurst)
*Day Trading with Short Term Price Patterns* (Crabel)
*Exceptional Trading: The Mind Game* (Roosevelt)
*Fibonacci Ratios with Pattern Recognition* (Pesavento)
*Futures Spread Trading: The Complete Guide* (Smith)
*Geometry of Markets* (Gilmore)
*Geometry of Stock Market Profits* (Jenkins)
*Harmonic Vibrations* (Pesavento)
*How to Trade in Stocks* (Livermore & Smitten)
*Hurst Cycles Course* (J.M. Hurst)
*Investing by the Stars* (Weingarten)
*Jesse Livermore: Speculator King* (Sarnoff)
*Magic of Moving Averages* (Lowry)
*Market Rap: The Odyssey of a Still-Struggling Commodity Trader* (Collins)
*Pit Trading: Do You Have the Right Stuff?* (Hoffman & Baccetti)
*Planetary Harmonics of Speculative Markets* (Pesavento)
*Point & Figure Charting* (Aby)
*Point & Figure Charting: Commodity and Stock Trading Techniques* (Zieg)
*Profitable Grain Trading* (Ainsworth)
*Profitable Patterns for Stock Trading* (Pesavento)
*Short-Term Trading with Price Patterns* (Harris)
*Stock Market Trading Systems* (Appel & Hitschler)
*Stock Patterns for Day Trading* (Rudd)
*Stock Patterns for Day Trading 2* (Rudd)
*Stock Patterns for Day Trading Home Study Course* (Rudd)
*Stock Trading Techniques Based on Price Patterns* (Harris)
*Study Helps in Point & Figure Techniques* (Wheelan)
*Technically Speaking* (Wilkinson)
*Technical Trading Systems for Commodities and Stocks* (Patel)
*The Amazing Life of Jesse Livermore: World's Greatest Stock Trader* (Smitten)
*The Opening Price Principle: The Best Kept Secret on Wall Street* (Pesavento)
*The Professional Commodity Trader* (Kroll)
*The Taylor Trading Technique* (Taylor)
*The Traders* (Kleinfeld)
*The Trading Rule That Can Make You Rich** (Dobson)
*Trading Secrets of the Inner Circle* (Goodwin)
*Trading S&P Futures and Options* (Lloyd)
*Twelve Habitudes of Highly Successful Traders* (Roosevelt)
*Understanding Bollinger Bands* (Dobson)
*Understanding Fibonacci Numbers* (Dobson)
*Viewpoints of a Commodity Trader* (Longstreet)
*Wall Street Ventures & Adventures Through Forty Years* (Wyckoff)
*Winning Market Systems* (Appel)